I Spoke to You

Before I Formed You

Melissa Hardy

Copyright © 2022 *Melissa Hardy*

Scripture quotations marked "AMP" are taken from the Amplified® Bible, Copyright © 1954, 1958, 1962, 1964, 1965, 1987 by The Lockman Foundation. Used by permission. Works using Amplified Bible, Classic Edition quotations must include one of the following copyright notices (whichever one is most appropriate): Scripture taken from the Amplified Bible (AMPCE), Copyright © 1954, 1958, 1962, 1964, 1965, 1987 by The Lockman Foundation. Used by permission. Scripture quota-tions marked CSB®, are taken from the Christian Standard Bible®, Copyright © 2017 by Holman Bi-ble Publishers. Used by permission. Christian Standard Bible®, and CSB® are federally registered trademarks of Holman Bible Publishers. Taken from the HOLY BIBLE: EASY-TO-READ VERSION © 2001 by World Bible Translation Center, Inc. and used by permission. Scripture quotations marked "ESV" are from the ESV Bible® (The Holy Bible, English Standard Version®), copyright © 2001 by Crossway Bibles, a publishing ministry of Good News Publishers. Used by permission. All rights reserved. Scripture quotations marked HCSB®, are taken from the Holman Christian Standard Bible®, Copy-right © 1999, 2000, 2002, 2003, 2009 by Holman Bible Publishers. Used by permission. HCSB® is a federally registered trademark of Holman Bible Publishers Scripture quotations marked "KJV" are taken from the Holy Bible, King James Version (Public Domain). Scriptures marked NIV are taken from the NEW INTERNATIONAL VERSION (NIV): Scripture taken from THE HOLY BIBLE, NEW INTERNA-TIONAL VERSION ®. Copyright© 1973, 1978, 1984, 2011 by Biblica, Inc.™. Used by permission of Zondervan. Scriptures marked NLT are taken from the HOLY BIBLE, NEW LIVING TRANSLATION (NLT): Scriptures taken from the HOLY BIBLE, NEW LIVING TRANSLATION, Copyright© 1996, 2004, 2007 by Tyndale House Foundation. Used by permission of Tyndale House Publishers, Inc., Carol Stream, Illi-nois 60188. All rights reserved. Used by permission. Scripture quotations marked "NKJV" are taken from the New King James Version. Copyright © 1982 by Thomas Nelson, Inc. Used by permission. All rights reserved. Bible text from the New King James Version® is not to be reproduced in copies or otherwise by any means except as permitted in writing by Thomas Nelson, Inc., Attn: Bible Rights and Permissions, P.O. Box 141000, Nashville, TN 37214-1000. Scripture quotations marked "MSG" or "The Message" are taken from The Message. Copyright 1993, 1994, 1995, 1996, 2000, 2001, 2002. Used by permission of NavPress Publishing Group. Scripture quotations marked "TPT" are from The Passion Translation®. Copyright © 2017, 2018 by Passion & Fire Ministries, Inc. Used by permission. All rights reserved. No part of this document may be reproduced or transmitted in any form or by any means, electronic, mechanical, photocopying, recording, or otherwise, without prior written permission of the author.

I SPOKE TO YOU
Before I Formed You

Melissa Hardy
i.spoke.to.you.beloved@gmail.com

ISBN 978-1-949826-56-2

Printed in the USA.
All rights reserved

Published by: EAGLES GLOBAL BOOKS | Frisco, Texas
In conjunction with the 2022 Eagles Authors Course
Cover & interior designed by DestinedToPublish.com

Disclaimer

"I SPOKE TO YOU: Before I Formed You and Placed You in Your Mother's Womb" is a Faith-based Book that stresses Biblical values and principles from a Christ-centered foundation.

This book is not therapy or a medical treatment. "I SPOKE TO YOU" does not diagnose or treat any medical or psychological condition. The information provided in this Book is for informational purposes only and is not a substitute for professional medical advice, diagnosis, or treatment. Always consult with a qualified medical professional for diagnosis and treatment of health or mental concerns. All teachings, tools, and practices mentioned or shared in this Book are for informational purposes only.

Enrolling in any online or in-person programs offered through Melissa Hardy's "I SPOKE TO YOU," whether in group or private sessions; reading any materials provided or suggested; viewing any videos; or interacting with Melissa Hardy via comments, virtual, email, telephone, directly, or any other form of communication does not constitute receiving treatment from or entering into a therapeutic relationship with Melissa Hardy's "I SPOKE TO YOU" or with Melissa Hardy herself. Neither Melissa Hardy nor anyone employed by Melissa Hardy is responsible for any adverse effects resulting from your use of or reliance on any information or recommendations received through "I SPOKE TO YOU."

DEDICATION

This book is dedicated to

Papa God,

The Son,

The Holy Spirit,

The Church of the Lord Jesus Christ,

And to all my brothers and sisters.

Who will embrace an intimate journey of self-discovery and healing with Papa God?

Acknowledgments

To my first LOVE – My Papa God, My Big Brother Christ Jesus, and My Best Friend the Holy Spirit.

~ This book is YOUR doorway to reach the LOST and the BROKEN HEARTED.

~ This book is YOUR key to equipping the Body of Christ for the work of the ministry.

~ This book is YOUR heartbeat for YOUR Beloved Bride, The Church.

It is an honor and privilege to serve as your Fire-Branded Scribe.

To my second LOVE – My husband Rodney Hardy, who has held my hand throughout the birthing journey of "I SPOKE TO YOU." His listening ear, anointed comments, fire-branded encouragement, and countless prayers have been invaluable. When I wanted to give up, he lovingly pointed me back to the calling on my life as a Prophet and Healer to the Nations. He is my gift from God, who I treasure deeply. I love you, Prophet Fire Warrior!

To my third LOVES – My Spiritual Parents, Pastors Kenneth and Cynthia Barbour, who have provided countless hours of spiritual counsel and unwavering encouragement, and who extended their faith to the birthing of "I SPOKE TO YOU." I love you, Mom and Pops!

To my fourth LOVES – My Faithful Prayer Warriors, Apostle Katrina Carter, Evangelist Keshia Freeland, Prophet Renee Murdock, Minister Evelyn Rivera, the Eagles International Training Institute Authors, my Publisher, Mrs. Marilyn Alexander, and my Coach, Ms. Kara May; who warred in the spirit for the birthing of "I SPOKE TO YOU."

Much love to the Warring Warriors!

Foreword

My Beloved,

I long for you to feel MY Heart Beat...

To feel MY Breath upon you...

Come and Commune with ME...

Oh, How I long to spend time with you, MY Beloved...

It is the thing I desire most, for you to be in MY Presence...

That you may feel the full Essence of MY Love for you...

It is from this place of deep love that "I SPOKE TO YOU" before I formed you and placed you in your Mother's womb...

It is from this place of deep love that I created you for MY Pleasure and MY Glory...

MELISSA HARDY

*I created you to duplicate ME on Earth ~
Come and enter into MY Presence...*

And hear ME whisper the very words "I SPOKE TO YOU" (BEFORE YOUR CREATION) – before I formed you and placed you in your Mother's womb...

I Love You, Papa God.

Endorsements

'I Spoke to You,' will encourage, build up and give insight into the prophetic revelations of how the Holy Spirit confirms your calling, gifts, and talents. Prophet Melissa has opened her heart to share how God is walking with her. We are excited about how individuals will go on their identity, healing, and transformational journey. Being profitable for the Kingdom of God. Remember always that life is a process.

Pastors Kenneth and Cynthia Barbour

If you have ever asked the question, "who am I?" and still do not know the answer, this book is a must-read. Melissa has shared intimate parts of her life to help others discover theirs. She calls us to go to the Father, who has all the answers. By reading 'I Spoke to You,' you will be unlocked and open to receive all God has for you.

Prophet Renee Murdock

TESTIMONY

Who Am I? Why Am I Here? What Is My Calling or Purpose in Life?

I spent years searching for the answers to these questions. I would wonder and ask myself these questions over and over. There was such a deep-seated desire to know my calling and purpose in life. I looked for these answers in others and even read many Christian self-help books hoping to find answers, but to no avail – I found no answers.

In 2017, I heard a message on the simplicity of uncovering my calling, purpose, and identity in Papa God. The speaker simply stated that I should ask Papa God the following question: "Papa God, what did You say to me before You made me and placed me in my Mother's womb?" At the end of the message, the speaker simply said, "Only the Creator (Papa God) can define their creation (YOU)!"

This message was engrafted in my heart, and it stirred a burning desire to hear the very words Papa God "SPOKE TO ME" before He formed me and placed me in my Mother's womb. This message changed my life forever! Something deep within me longed to hear Papa God's very words, so I started asking Him the question, "Daddy, what did You say to me before You made me and placed me in my Mother's womb?" I continued to ask Him this question until He responded to me early one morning. Papa God woke me up around 3:00 a.m. and said, "Today is the day I will reveal those very words to you, My Daughter." He then instructed me to turn on the recorder on my cell phone and to begin to pray and worship... AND THEN...

Over my next three hours of praying, worshipping, and hearing His audible voice, Papa God spoke the following:

> "For you are great in my sight – I have made you great, while you may be small in stature – you are bigger than you can ever imagine. I will use you to deliver millions of people from the hands of the enemy. Everything you do is tied to delivering MY people. Everything you have been through is for MY glory. People will be delivered through your touch and by the words you speak, you are a deliverer to The Nations!
>
> I have told you before, you are a conveyer belt from heaven. You are MY philanthropist and I will entrust millions of dollars to you for My Kingdom. The money I am giving you is to create ways to deliver people and to build places for them to be delivered to. I am commanding you to deliver MY people – To raise up the desolate! You are mighty in the Great Commission, and you are one of MY generals.

I SPOKE TO YOU BEFORE I FORMED YOU

You are MY mouthpiece – you are MY prophet! Your great name will be known as MY FIRE, MY secret weapon – FIRE, FIRE, FIRE is who you are. I call you MY Fire, MY Deliverer, MY Prophet, and MY Philanthropist.

Because of the great mandate on your life, you must be able to see through MY lenses. You must be able to hear what I hear, to sense and feel what I do. You must be able to see everyone as I do. You must be able to flow between two worlds (the supernatural and the physical). You must live and operate from the supernatural – NO FEAR, only courage and boldness. It is through MY power and anointing that you will freely flow – it is only through ME. I am the key to the revelation, power, anointing, fire, healing, prophecies, deliverance, and wealth that will flow through you. Your names are:

~ Consuming Fire – Everything you touch will be consumed with MY FIRE. MY FIRE changes and transforms things, it heals, it destroys, and it purifies.

~ Fire Bug – You will start FIRES everywhere you go – that's what FIRE BUGS do.

~ Diamond – You have been through the FIRE your whole life, and it's time for you to shine.

~ Glitter Fire – When diamonds come out of the FIRE, they glitter and shine. I will use you to help others through the process of purification.

I love you just the way you are – I will develop you into what pleases ME and not others. You are different, quirky, and unique. Just DO and BE who I say you are – just move and flow with ME."

At the end of my Daddy encounter, I felt like the light switch within me had been turned on. At that very moment, I knew that I knew who I was. It was as if I had been in the dark my whole life – walking around aimless and lost. But now, there is no question – I am Papa God's Prophet, Healer, and Philanthropist!

As I walked in the freedom of my Kingdom Calling and Identity, Papa God began to walk me down memory lane – reliving the past 50 years of my life. He shared the devil's strategies to assassinate the calling on my life. The devil's manifested plan over the years included:

> The Spirit of Infirmity – for over 30 years, I experienced illness after illness, which resulted in me claiming 42 illnesses in my military retirement disability entitlement.

> The Spirit of Death – numerous car accidents (neck and back injuries); a bike accident where I was thrown 50 feet and landed face first in the concrete (jaw injury, and knocking out all my teeth); a military accident where I fell eight feet and landed on my head (resulting in Traumatic Brain Injury).

> Molestation – At a very young age, I was molested by two male family members.

> Spirit of Hatred – I witnessed my father physically, emotionally, and verbally abuse my mother for over 50 years; my sibling and I experienced emotional and verbal abuse at the hand of our father; and I experienced emotional and verbal abuse by my ex-husband.

Post-Traumatic Stress Disorder (PTSD) – I battled with PTSD as a result of the childhood violence, molestation, military combat, and sexual harassment which manifested in depression, anxiety, and alcohol abuse.

Sexual Harassment – Throughout my military and federal government career, I have experienced incidents of sexual harassment from people ranging from peers to senior officials.

All of these assassination strategies resulted in me:

Living in a CAVE of low self-esteem, unworthiness, self-doubt, and not having a voice.

Hiding behind the MASK of PERFECTIONISM – I expected perfection in myself and others.

Living a life as a MASTER CONTROLLER – I believed that if I could control everything and everyone around me, nothing bad would or could happen.

While the strategies, tactics, and plans of the devil were beyond extreme in my life, he had already lost his battle of assassination before it begun. And before God "SPOKE TO ME" and formed me and placed me in my Mother's womb, I had already victoriously completed my Kingdom Calling on Earth.

My Story in Heaven was complete before it began on Earth.

"I SPOKE TO YOU" is my very own
story and walk with God.

Encountering God

Throughout "I SPOKE TO YOU," you will be encouraged to encounter Papa God through Fasting, Prayer, Selah, Prophetic Activations, Worship, and Soaking. It is through these moments of time that your relationship with Papa God will blossom into a beautiful garden. For some of you, it will be a garden of daisies or roses, and for others, it may be a garden of exotic flowers. Whatever lies in your garden, know that it is Papa God Inspired and Spoken from before time. May you embrace the journey of discovering the garden before you – your Kingdom Identity?

Garden Gate

Keys For Unlocking Papa God Encounters

ENCOUNTERS WITH PAPA GOD AND WITH GOD

*"My Beloved, throughout 'I SPOKE TO YOU,' you will encounter Me as your Papa God and Father, and as your God. As your Papa God and Father, I am in communication with you from a posture of intimate relationship – a deep relationship only shared between you and Me. As your God, I am communicating from an authoritative posture – as your King of Kings – as the Creator of all things. I have placed special emphasis on key words or phrases, which are either all CAPITALIZED or **BOLDED** – as you read 'I SPOKE TO YOU,' take time to Selah these key words or phrases. Throughout 'I SPOKE TO YOU,' you will read special love letters and messages from Me to you.*

I love you, Papa God."

FASTING AND PRAYER

Fasting is intentionally (deliberately, purposely, and with intent) setting aside time to spend with God. Fasting must be accompanied with prayer, or else it's just a time of denying oneself. Fasting does not move nor change God; however, fasting changes you and postures you to hear from God. The Holy Spirit may direct you to fast and provide you with specific instructions. Or you may be led to fast on your own for various reasons; for example, you may want to develop a deeper relationship with God through reading His Word, and in doing so, you may choose to fast from television for a specific time frame, replacing the time you would spend watching television with reading the Word of God. It's during these times of desiring more – going deeper – that you will encounter God in new ways.

Fasting and praying will posture you for new levels of intimacy and transformation. Additional benefits include spiritual growth, purifying the heart and mind, breaking habits and spiritual bondages, and improving physical health. Most importantly, fasting quiets your heart to hear God's voice.

From a traditional standpoint, when it comes to fasting, most people fast from food for a specific time frame. However, I would recommend always following the leading of the Holy Spirit with reference to the type and duration of your fast. The Holy Spirit knows exactly what you need at that very moment in time.

Fasting doesn't have to be complicated, and no two fasts are identical. Every time you enter into a fasting period, you are personally in a different paragraph or chapter of your life. Therefore, while the Holy Spirit may instruct you to fast from television for several fasts in a row, your God encounters will be different every time.

SELAH

"Moments of Reflection Pertaining to the Word of God"

Selah is a Hebrew word referring to an intentional and purposeful pause for reflection as one reads the Word of God. Often in times of pausing, God will give you a revelation that changes your perspective, bringing you closer to Him. Selah postures you to hear His voice and to be in His presence.

The word Selah can be found 74 times in the Poetic Books of Psalms and Habakkuk. It's very interesting that God would choose to place the word Selah in His poetic books, as it is through the poetic books that one can glean revelation from the very essence of God's heart for the Nations, His people, and us as individuals.

In Psalm 139:13-14 (CSB), we hear David having a conversation with God: "For you created my inmost being; you knit me together in my mother's womb. For it was you who created my inward parts; you knit me together in my mother's womb. I will praise you because I have been remarkably and wondrously made. SELAH!"

Take a moment and make this scripture personal by inserting your name. Close your eyes and repeat the personalized scripture slowly three times, allowing yourself to enter into His presence for 15 minutes through SELAH.

"For it was YOU who created my, (Name), inward parts, YOU knit me, (Name), together in my Mother's womb. I, (Name), will praise YOU because I, (Name), have been remarkably and wondrously made. SELAH!"

As you were reflecting on Papa God creating every one of your inward parts and placing you in your Mother's womb, and on being fearfully and wonderfully made by the King of Kings, what came to mind? Did you receive a new revelation?

Journal: _____

_____

_____

_____

_____

_____

Taking the time to reflect on the Word of God opens your heart to hear what God wants to say to you personally. May your journey through "I SPOKE TO YOU" and your life chapters be full of many Selah encounters with God.

PROPHETIC ACTIVATIONS

Prophetic Activation is a SUPERNATURAL ACT that releases the manifested power of God from the Kingdom realm into the Earthly realm. A prophetic activation is done under the direction of the Holy Spirit and aligns with what God is doing in the spiritual realm. It opens the passage for God's presence, power, and victory to flow, creating breakthrough in the spiritual realm with manifested results in the natural. A prophetic act is not a man-made formula or technique that you can carelessly follow to produce change. You may find it challenging at times to fully describe or rationalize a prophetic act with your own human mind. Your prophetic activations are you communicating with Papa God on a whole new level of faith and trust, which results in your relationship blossoming to new heights. Prophetic activations will also encourage you, strengthen you, and help you grow in all areas of your personal life. God is not asking you to understand everything He does; He just desires for you to trust and surrender yourself unto Him. Are you willing to let go and let God? Anything can happen when you partner with and obey God!

Just imagine the Israelites standing on the banks of the Red Sea, watching the Egyptian Army approaching – with no way of escape. Fear gripped the Nation of Israel! But Moses cried out to God for guidance and protection, and he heard the voice of God. In obedience, Moses raised his staff (a prophetic act/activation), and God moved mightily by parting the Red Sea. Through this prophetic act, the Nation of Israel (the Israelites) was provided a route of escape from the Egyptian Army.

Examples of Prophetic Acts:

- ~ Cutting the air with a pair of scissors to gesture the cutting away of a undesirable issue in your life or others
- ~ Planting a tree to signify new life and growth (personally or for a city, region, or state)
- ~ Praying over your home, church, or city while waving a flag
- ~ The possibilities are endless. Why? Because our God is a God of endless possibilities!

Remember, the key is to always seek God prior to commencing a Prophetic Activation or Act:

- ~ God, what is the issue at hand?
- ~ God, do you want me to do a prophetic activation to facilitate change?

~ If so, what prophetic activation do YOU desire?

It is never recommended to engage in a prophetic act that does not come from God.

PRAISE, PROPHETIC WORSHIP, AND SOAKING

The words Praise and Worship are used interchangeably; however, they do not mean the same thing. Yes, praise and worship complement one another, but it is important to know the difference between the two.

Praise is a form of giving thanks, of recognizing and appreciating God for all that He has done for you. God commands you to praise Him through His Word.

> Psalm 100:4 (NKJV): *"Enter into His gates with thanksgiving, And into His courts with praise. Be thankful to Him, and bless His name."*

> Psalm 69:30 (NKJV): *"I will praise the name of God with a song, and will magnify Him with thanksgiving."*

Worship is an expression of love, devotion, and wonder, which is only reserved for God. God desires and longs for you to seek Him in worship! It's in this place of worship that you enter into His very presence.

> John 4:23 (NKJV): *"But the hour is coming, and now is, when the true worshipers will worship the Father in spirit and truth; for the Father is seeking such to worship Him."*

1 Chronicles 16:29 (NKJV): *"Give to the Lord the glory due His name; bring an offering, and come before Him. Oh, worship the Lord in the beauty of holiness!"*

Prophetic Worship is a place of being lost in God's presence. It is a place of deep intimacy between you and Papa God. It is a time to experience the very essence of His love for you. When you enter into prophetic worship, you are very sensitive to what the Holy Spirit is saying or doing in that very moment. It is during this time of worship that you will begin to decree and declare what God is saying over your situation and life.

Soaking is a term used to refer to being at peace in the presence of God. As you rest in His presence, you soak in the very essence of who God is and who He created you to be. It's a posture you take for the sole purpose of spending express time with God. Soaking is creating a space for God to encounter you. As you wait upon the Lord, you will begin to hear His voice and experience who He is. In Psalm 46:10 (NIV), God says, "Be still, and know that I am God; I will be exalted among the nations, I will be exalted in the earth."

Praise, Worship, Prophetic Worship, and Soaking must be an essential part of your daily walk and relationship with God. You should desire to live from a place of thanksgiving and gratefulness, and long to be in your Father's presence from day to day.

Remember, as you continue reading "I SPOKE TO YOU," it's important to use caution when selecting your own musical selections for praise, worship, prophetic worship, or soaking.

Allowing yourself to be led by The Holy Spirit is always best. For a list of musical selections see Appendix, Prophet Worship and Soaking YouTube Playlist.

DECREES, DECLARATIONS & PROCLAMATIONS

Today's church and many Kingdom Citizens use the words "decrees," "declarations," and "proclamations" interchangeably, together, or in context as meaning the same. Why is this? In the church there is a lack of Biblical teaching on these terms and how to effectively use them to produce manifested results in our lives. However, there are many books and articles available for you to gain a greater understanding and insight into their meanings, but here are simplified definitions of each.

A DECREE is an official, formal, and authoritative order which may be enforced by law; as a verb, it means to command something, to ordain something or someone, or to make a final decision. God has granted you the power and authority to issue an official unchangeable order or command. Job 22:28 (AMP) states, *"You will also decide and decree a thing, and it will be established for you; and the light [of God's favor] will shine upon your ways."*

A DECLARATION announces full support of something or makes our position clear. God has given you the choice to align with heaven and make your position clear through your own personal declarations.

A PROCLAMATION is an announcement made publicly; it removes any doubt and affirms your agreement and position, and it strengthens your own faith and spiritual posture. God has given you the ability to proclaim on Earth what has already been decreed in Heaven.

Let's make a simple decree, declaration, and proclamation of God's favor over your family.

I **DECREE** the favor of God upon the (Family Last Name) family. This decree establishes and aligns your family with God's favor and rejects anything that may come against His favor.

I **DECLARE** in prayer, Lord, You said in Your Word that Your favor is upon the (last name) family. I stand in full agreement with Your Word and Your favor, this is our unmovable position: Your favor is upon the (last name) family! And nothing will move nor separate my family from Your favor.

I **PROCLAIM** that the favor of God is upon the (last name) family. Your public announcement allows you to walk in confidence and to celebrate God's favor. Your proclamation also binds and paralyzes the plans of the enemy against your family.

The Word of God is powerful, transformational, and will change your life. Your DECREES, DECLARATIONS, AND PROCLAMATIONS bring you into alignment with what has already taken place in Heaven. You have the power to release what is in Heaven into the Earth. You, Beloved, are living in the days of an open Heaven – Oh, how God desires for you to decree, declare, and proclaim His Word in every area of your life. You are a Kingdom Citizen destined to live from a Kingdom Posture (an Open Heaven).

JOURNALING

Journaling is a way to keep a written, permanent account of your spiritual growth and your intimate conversations with God.

How to Journal: There is no one right way to journal. You may elect to journal daily in one journal or have several journals for different topics. You may choose to journal using pens with different color ink. Writing your thoughts in one color and God's thoughts in another color allows you to quickly locate God's heart (words) throughout your journal. You may choose to write in red ink when you're mad or frustrated, or green when you're happy – this will allow you to locate your emotions throughout your journal. You can also feel free to draw in your journal – drawing helps you connect with your words. One fun thing about journaling is finding a journal that you like. My favorite is a leather journal with the Tree of Life stamped into the leather. I love the feel and smell of leather – there is something raw about leather, just like my written thoughts. The Tree of Life reminds me that there is life in mine and Papa God's words. The key is selecting what works best for you and how you will use your journals in the future.

Benefits of Journaling:

- ~ Journaling helps you pay attention to God, both in hearing and in responding to Him.
- ~ It helps you to grow closer to God and see your personal growth over time.
- ~ It forces you to slow down and process what's going on around you.

- It helps you put your feelings into words or words into feelings.
- Writing to God can often lead to the root(s) behind your feelings.
- It heals toxic emotions, guilt, and grief.
- It helps you deal with the past (seeing yourself in the Word, dealing with negative thoughts, and forgiving yourself).
- It assists you in setting future goals and plans.
- You can be your authentic self – God loves your passion, so just let go and be you.
- Most importantly, you are capturing God's heart for you in words.

Beloved, you will need to purchase a journal to capture yours and Papa God's thoughts, as you journey through "I SPOKE TO YOU."

Table of Contents

Prophetic Introduction xxxiii

Section I: Unveiling God's Word 1
    Chapter 1: Hearing His Voice 3
    Chapter 2: Before Your Creation 21

Section II: Called For Such A Time As Now! 29
    Chapter 3 : You Have Been Chosen 31
    Chapter 4: "I Am". 47
    Chapter 5: Living from the Throne Room 63

Section III: A Time Of Healing. 75
    Chapter 6: Strongholds 77
    Chapter 7: A Choice To Heal. 87

Section IV : Cultivating Your Relationship With God 97
    Chapter 8: Through Dying To Self. 99
    Chapter 9: Through Intimacy. 109
    Chapter 10: Through The Fruit Of The Spirit. 119

Section V: The Birthing Room 131
    Chapter 11: Preparing For Birth. 133
    Chapter 12: It's Time 145

Section VI: Generations To Come 157
    Chapter 13: Building Legacy 159
    Chapter 14: Passing Through Generations 175

Appendix
    Prophetic Worship and Soaking Playlist. 187
    Conclusion 201

Prophetic Introduction

I SPOKE TO YOU is not a self-help book. This book is the very voice and breathe of Papa God – His divine plan for every reader. It holds the blueprint of the architect who created you. Papa God's words hold the keys to your very existence. His words answer your questions of "Why am I here?" and "Who Am I?" This journey of "I SPOKE TO YOU" is about connecting you to the voice of Papa God – to that place of intimacy between you and Papa God, a place that only belongs to you and Papa God.

Before Papa God formed you and placed you in your Mother's womb, He spoke to you, My Beloved.

~ God spoke your divine purpose

~ God spoke your callings and gifting's

~ God called you by your heavenly name

> *"Before I formed you* (BELOVED) *in the womb I knew you [and approved of you as My chosen instrument], And before you were born I consecrated you [to Myself as My own]; I have appointed you* (BELOVED) *as a prophet to the nations* (YOUR SPECIFIC CALLING).*"* (Jeremiah 1:5, AMP, alterations mine)

> *"…for He* (PAPA GOD) *delivered you and saved you and called you with a holy calling [a calling that leads to a consecrated life – a life set apart – a life of purpose], not because of your works [or because of any personal merit – you could do nothing to earn this], but because of His own purpose and grace [His amazing, undeserved favor] which was granted to you in Christ Jesus before the world began [eternal ages ago]…"* (2 Timothy 1:9, AMP, alterations mine)

AND THEN, Beloved, You Spoke to Papa God Your Yes (Agreement)! Aligning yourself to your purpose, callings, and gifting's – your Kingdom Identity.

AND THEN, Papa God placed you in your Mother's womb and sent you to Earth, for His Glory! Papa God sent you to Earth to walk out your calling – His legacy, which is a manifestation of Kingdom history – to relive what has already taken place in Heaven.

> *"That which is has already been, and that which will be has already been, for God seeks what has passed by [so that history repeats itself]."* (Ecclesiastes 3:15, AMP)

God is the beginning (THE ALPHA – THE CREATOR) and the end (THE OMEGA – THE FINISHER). Therefore, everything on earth has already been created, executed, and completed in Heaven. God requires you to partner with Him – you are a conduit (a channel, canal, pipeline, and outlet) from Heaven to Earth, For His Glory!

> Prophetic Message from Papa God: *"My Beloved, as you read My Words throughout 'I SPOKE TO YOU,' you will supernaturally and spiritually come alive. Your spirit, soul and natural man will intertwine and become one IN ME and WITH ME. And I will stir and ignite the fire within you so that I may use you as a vessel of light for My Glory. So, surrender yourself to what I have to say in the pages to come. I am excited to see the realization of your true identity come to life. For the time has come for Me to resuscitate you back to life. Oh, how I have waited for this moment in time to give you the Breath of Life. Come, My Beloved, take My Hand and Follow Me.*
>
> *I Love You, Papa God."*

Beloved, "I SPOKE TO YOU: Before I Formed You" was birthed from prophetic revelation received from Papa God.

Section I
Unveiling God's Word

"You are a manifestation of MY Spoken Words, Love Papa God." – Melissa Hardy

"Only the Creator (God) can define their creation (YOU)!" – Melissa Hardy

I Spoke to You

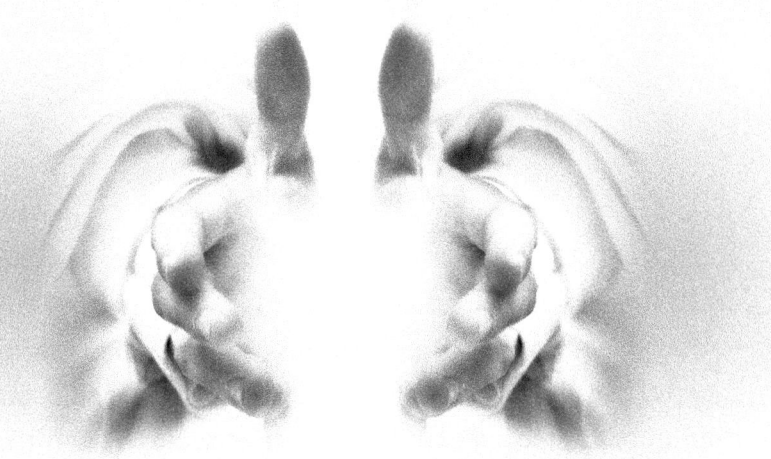

CHAPTER 1

HEARING HIS VOICE

QUOTE

"There is nothing more powerful, impactful, and life changing than hearing the voice of your Creator, Papa God." – Melissa Hardy

LOVE NOTE

"My Beloved, Oh how I long for times of intimacy with you – Times that belong to YOU and ME only. Moments where OUR hearts are intertwined as one and MY VOICE, MY HEARTBEAT for you is flowing freely. It's in this place of intimacy that you will fully know how much I desire to be in YOUR presence and how much I love you.

I love you, Papa God."

THE MESSAGE

"I SPOKE TO YOU" teaches you to hear the Voice of God and discover your True Kingdom Identity. Hearing God's voice may not be something you experience on a normal basis, whether audibly, visually, through dream and visions, through colors or nature, or any other way God chooses to speak to you individually. The key to hearing the Voice of God is that it requires you to enter into His presence. It is in these intimate encounters that God reveals His Heart towards you.

You can experience God encounters through times of fasting, praying, worshipping, soaking, prophetic activations, journaling, and reflecting (Selah) in His presence. Encountering God comes from a deep desire to want to know Him more. This only happens when you spend time with Him, setting aside time to actively listen to what He is saying.

Encountering God these days is no different than it was for our brothers and sisters in the Bible. Those who truly knew God spent time with Him and dedicated themselves to encountering Him by:

"Discerning Every Aspect of His Very Being,"

"Hearing His Voice and Heart,"

"Surrendering Themselves to Be Transformed and Fashioned by Him."

Just as God spoke to them, He longs to speak to you. Close your eyes and imagine yourself with Moses at the burning bush, listening to God speak of Moses' Kingdom assignment: *"So now I am sending you (Moses) to Pharaoh. Go! Lead my people, the Israelites, out of Egypt (out of bondage)."* (Exodus 3:10, ERV, alterations mine). Can you imagine being charged with delivering a whole Nation of people? Yes, you! Maybe you're called to deliver a neighborhood, city, region, state, or territory.

Or imagine yourself in Joseph's dream as he listens to the angel of the Lord encourage him not to be afraid to take Mary as his wife, and Mary's Kingdom assignment of birthing the Savior of the World (Matthew 1:20-25). The angel of the Lord was also speaking of Joseph's Kingdom assignment indirectly. By taking Mary as his wife, Joseph would take on the responsibility to provide for and protect Mary and Jesus. God was entrusting them with the parental responsibility for His Beloved Son. Talk about a major obligation – raising Jesus, the Son of God, and the Savior of Mankind!

CAN YOU IMAGINE how Moses and Joseph must have felt in the very presence of God, the King of Kings, and to hear God speak directly to them about their Kingdom assignments and Godly identity? WOW! The question "Can you imagine?" is a Selah moment – a time to pause for reflection. Often in times of pausing, God will give you a revelation that changes your perspective, bringing you closer to Him. Selah postures you to hear His voice and to be in His presence. You are encouraged to take moments of Selah throughout your journey of discovery.

Revealing your purpose in life (callings, gifting's, identity, true authenticity) is quite a simple process. However, society, theologians, and countless authors have made this journey of self-discovery seem complicated and time consuming. The majority of books pertaining to this topic never lead their readers to the very Creator, God! But in time, and through this journey, you will clearly hear the Voice of God and know without a shadow of doubt who you are in God and your purpose for life.

THE FOUNDATION OF HEARING GOD'S VOICE

Before you begin your journey of hearing God's voice, you need to go back to the foundation of creation. IN THE BEGINNING, God (known as "The Trinity" – Father, Son, and Holy Spirit) created man in His very image. In Genesis 1:26-27 (AMP), we see the Father, Son, and Holy Spirit engaging in a visionary conversation about creating man:

> *"Then God said, "Let Us (Father, Son, Holy Spirit) make man in Our image, according to Our likeness [not physical, but a spiritual personality and moral likeness]; and let them have complete authority over the fish of the sea, the birds of the air, the cattle, and over the entire earth, and over everything that creeps and crawls on the earth. So God created man in His own image, in the image and likeness of God He created him; male and female He created them."*

And since you are created in His very image, you were created with the desire (yearning, craving, and longing) and ability (capacity) to communicate with the Father, Son, and Holy Spirit. This isn't something reserved for those who serve in leadership roles within the church. No, this is your inherited birthright to communicate with your Creator – Your Father. From a natural perspective, you communicate with your birth mother and father, listening to their words of love, affirmation, guidance, and correction. Your heavenly

Father so desires for you to have free-flowing conversations with Him day and night.

The continuation of THE BEGINNING: after creating man, God SPOKE TO THEM their Kingdom CALLING and PURPOSE.

> *"And God blessed them and said to them, **Be fruitful, multiply, and fill the earth**, and **subdue it** [using all its vast resources in the service of God and man]; and **have dominion over** the fish of the sea, the birds of the air, and over every living creature that moves upon the earth."* (Genesis 1:28, AMPC)

> *"God blessed them: **Prosper! Reproduce! Fill Earth! Take charge!** Be responsible for fish in the sea and birds in the air, for every living thing that moves on the face of Earth.'"* (Genesis 1:28, MSG)

And then God placed them in the Garden of Eden.

> *"So the Lord God took the man [He had made] and settled him in the Garden of Eden to cultivate and keep it."* (Genesis 2:15, AMP)

God provided them with everything they needed to fulfill their Kingdom assignment.

> *"So God said, 'Behold, I have given you every plant yielding seed that is on the surface of the entire earth, and every tree which has fruit yielding seed; it shall be food for you; and to all the animals on the earth and to every bird of the air and to everything that moves on the ground – to everything in which there is the breath of life – I have given every green plant for food'; and it was so [because He commanded it]."* (Genesis 1:29-30, AMP)

God provided them with the Garden of Eden rules (instructions and guidelines).

> *"And the Lord God commanded the man, saying, 'You may freely (unconditionally) eat [the fruit] from every tree of the garden; but [only] from the tree of the knowledge (recognition) of good and evil you shall not eat, otherwise on the day that you eat from it, you shall most certainly die [because of your disobedience]."* (Genesis 2:16-17, AMP)

Life was good for Adam and Eve – they were fulfilling their Kingdom assignment, and they were freely communing with God (communicating, conversing, connecting, and feeling at one with God and in touch with God). Close your eyes and just imagine what it must have been like to live in paradise and to fellowship with God daily. Adam and Eve were living the dream life, and then they freely chose to disobey God's rules pertaining to the Tree of Knowledge. They allowed themselves to be tricked and deceived by Satan (the serpent), and they ate of the Tree of Knowledge.

> *"Now the serpent was more crafty (subtle, skilled in deceit) than any living creature of the field which the Lord God had made. And the serpent (Satan) said to the woman, 'Can it really be that God has said, "You shall not eat from any tree of the garden"?' And the woman said to the serpent, 'We may eat fruit from the trees of the garden, except the fruit from the tree which is in the middle of the garden. God said, "You shall not eat from it nor touch it, otherwise you will die."' But the serpent said to the woman, 'You certainly will not die! For God knows that on the day you eat from it your eyes will be opened [that is, you will have greater awareness], and*

you will be like God, knowing [the difference between] good and evil.' And when the woman saw that the tree was good for food, and that it was delightful to look at, and a tree to be desired in order to make one wise and insightful, she took some of its fruit and ate it; and she also gave some to her husband with her, and he ate. Then the eyes of the two of them were opened [that is, their awareness increased], and they knew that they were naked; and they fastened fig leaves together and made themselves coverings." (Genesis 3:3-7, AMP)

The Fall of Man – Adam and Eve lost everything! They were exiled from their home, stripped of their power, authority, and ability to communicate with God. Adam and Eve (you and I) are now spiritually dead – disconnected (separated, detached, cut off) from the very presence of God. Can you imagine how devastated Adam and Eve must have been? They went from intimate conversations to zero communication.

"And the Lord God said, 'Behold, the man has become like one of Us (Father, Son, Holy Spirit), knowing [how to distinguish between] good and evil; and now, he might stretch out his hand, and take from the tree of life as well, and eat [its fruit], and live [in this fallen, sinful condition] forever" – therefore the Lord God sent Adam away from the Garden of Eden, to till and cultivate the ground from which he was taken. So God drove the man out; and at the east of the Garden of Eden He [permanently] stationed the cherubim and the sword with the flashing blade which turned round and round [in every direction] to protect and guard the way (entrance, access) to the tree of life." (Genesis 3:22-24, AMP)

The Reconciliation of Man – God has reconciled you back to Him through Jesus Christ and restored your ability to communicate with Him.

> *"What we have seen and heard we also proclaim to you, so that you too may have fellowship [as partners] with us. And indeed our fellowship [which is a distinguishing mark of born-again believers] is with the Father, and with His Son Jesus Christ. We are writing these things to you so that our joy [in seeing you included] may be made complete [by having you share in the joy of salvation]."* (1 John 1:3-4, AMP)

The Revived Communication Process (Salvation) – Your communication with God is activated through a renewed spirit by accepting, believing in, and confessing Jesus Christ as the LORD of your life. If you have not received JESUS CHRIST as your LORD and SAVIOR, this is the very moment in time for you to return to your Heavenly Father. He is waiting for you with open arms; He is calling your name. Can you hear Him calling your name?

> *"My Beloved, I have been waiting for this very moment in time. Oh, How I have longed for you to return home – into MY loving arms. Before 'I SPOKE TO YOU' and placed you in your Mother's womb, I cradled you in MY arms. And on this day, I am rejoicing with all of Heaven that you have chosen ME. I am not concerned with your past failures or sin. Why? Because the Blood of My Beloved Son has already taken care of your past. All that awaits you is an eternal life with ME, and all your brothers and sisters in Heaven.*
>
> *I Love You, Papa God."*

WORSHIP – SURRENDERED HEART

"Amazing Grace" – recorded by Judy Collins, video by Gary Downey

PRAYER OF SALVATION

Lord Jesus, for too long I've kept you out of my life. I know that I am a sinner and that I cannot save myself. No longer will I close the door when I hear you knocking. By faith I gratefully receive your gift of salvation. I am ready to trust you as my Lord and Savior. Thank you, Lord Jesus, for coming to earth. I believe you are the Son of God who died on the cross for my sins and rose from the dead on the third day. Thank you for bearing my sins and giving me the gift of eternal life. I believe your words are true. Come into my heart, Lord Jesus, and be my Savior. Amen.

The Renewed Spirit – It is through your renewed spirit that you are able to hear the Voice of God, through the Holy Spirit, for no one knows the thoughts of God except the Holy Spirit.

> *"For what person knows the thoughts and motives of a man except the man's spirit within him? So also no one knows the thoughts of God except the Spirit of God. Now we have received, not the spirit of the world, but the [Holy] Spirit who is from God, so that we may know and understand the [wonderful] things freely given to us by God. We also speak of these things, not in words taught or supplied by human wisdom, but in those taught by the Spirit, combining and interpreting spiritual thoughts with spiritual words [for those being guided by the Holy Spirit]."* (1 Corinthians 2:11-13, AMP)

The Holy Spirit – You may have several questions when it comes to the Holy Spirit. For instance, who is the Holy Spirit, and what roles does the Holy Spirit play in your life? The term "Holy Spirit" comes from the Greek word *Parakletos*, which means "Helper."

The Holy Spirit is the Spirit of God, the third person of the Trinity (Father, Son, and Holy Spirit). Many people view the Holy Spirit as simply a supernatural power or a person of influence. The Holy Spirit's assignment is to navigate you through your journey on Earth – He is your "Helper."

The Father, Son, and the Holy Spirit are one; all three are unique and united in oneness – this is the most powerful and mysterious thing about the Trinity. You can say that each person is co-equal and co-eternal. The Holy Spirit's role complements the person and work of Jesus Christ our LORD and the eternal will of the Father.

All scripture is God-breathed and authored by the Holy Spirit: *"All Scripture is God-breathed [given by divine inspiration] and is profitable for instruction, for conviction [of sin], for correction [of error and restoration to obedience], for training in righteousness [learning to live in conformity to God's will, both publicly and privately—behaving honorably with personal integrity and moral courage]"* (2 Timothy 3:16, AMP). Through the divine inspiration of the Holy Spirit, natural men scribed what you know now as the Bible: *"No prophecy ever came from what some person wanted to say. But people were led by the Holy Spirit and spoke words from God"* (2 Peter 1:21, ERV).

The Holy Spirit sanctifies you (1 Corinthians 6:11) – He helps you to purge your sins and spiritually mature to become more Christlike. Sanctification is a lifelong process, which requires you to be daily dying to your old self in order to become who God created you to be.

Your goal is to become "Christlikeness," and this can only take place with the help of the Holy Spirit (2 Corinthians 3:18). Moses experienced God's glory and then reflected His glory. But you radiate the glory of God through seeing the Lord Jesus Christ in God's Word, which equals transformation.

The Holy Spirit will direct you in fulfilling your Kingdom assignment – the will of the Father. Throughout the Bible, we see example after example of the Holy Spirit directing people (Acts 8:29).

The Holy Spirit gives you gift(s) in order to empower you to accomplish the calling on your life (1 Corinthians 12:4-11).

The Holy Spirit imparts love; He pours God's love into your heart. God's love empowers you to handle difficult seasons in your life (Romans 5:3-5).

The Holy Spirit fills your soul with hope, that you will experience peace in all things (Romans 15:13).

The Holy Spirit is your teacher and provides you with wisdom and understanding (John 14:26).

The Holy Spirit is your prayer partner – when you don't know what to pray, the Holy Spirit knows just what needs to be said (Romans 8:26).

And lastly, the Holy Spirit will use you to evangelize to others, telling others about Jesus and the Kingdom of God. The very essence of HEARING GOD'S VOICE is to embrace what God has put inside of you and to be His instrument for Kingdom purpose!

My Story: After I received salvation at the age of 23, it took me years to learn how to hear the voice of Papa God for myself. Learning to hear His voice required relationship, and back then, I didn't view God as Papa God. He was God – the one who disciplined me when I made mistakes or sinned. My view was based on my dysfunctional relationship with my natural father, which I will share more in depth in chapter 8.

My inability to see God as a loving father – as My Papa God – resulted in me becoming codependent on others to hear for me. This codependency fueled my weakness to want to please people. As a people pleaser, I allowed others to hear from God for me and to guide my decision-making process. During these years, I made a lot of bad decisions, which severely impacted my immediate family members and others. Some of these relationships have taken years to repair and restore, and there are still a few I am personally working on. I also placed myself in the prison of unforgiveness, allowing the prison bars to hinder me from having healthy relationships not rooted in codependency. During my Christian Counseling process and attending Bible College, I slowly uncovered the root of codependency and Papa God healed this area of my life.

And as I healed, God became My Papa God – My Father – and I began chasing after Him as a little girl runs after her Daddy. And as I pursued Him through prayer, worship, and reading His Word, our relationship began to blossom. I would find myself in His presence, and He would begin to communicate with me through visions, through dreams, and audibly. During our times of intimacy, Papa God would share His heart towards me, and He would tell me how much He loved me. I love being in His presence so much... I became a chaser of His presence... and then I transitioned to Living from His presence.

Beloved, the more you pursue Papa God, the more your relationship will blossom with beautiful love notes from your Papa God.

ACTIVATION

Let's take a moment to practice Selah. Find somewhere peaceful and quietly reflect on the questions below:

Question 1: Why were you created and sent to Earth?

Question 2: What area of responsibility or ministry has God placed within you?

Question 3: To where (neighborhood, city, region, state, territory, or Nation) and to whom (what group of people) is God sending you?

Question 4: What is your Kingdom assignment?

Once you've answered these questions, you will need to write down your responses in your journal.

These questions, along with others you may have, can be quite overwhelming. Take a moment to release the peace of God that already exists within you. Close your eyes and take three deep breaths – hold each one for 15 seconds and then slowly exhale. The very breath of life God blew into your nostrils when you became a living human being is the very same breath of air you just inhaled. Your Creator is the very same God who will answer your questions and empower you to fulfill your Kingdom assignment. If God has placed something within you, then the responsibility for its manifestation falls on HIM. Your job is to know and understand who you are in HIM and to live a surrendered life of obedience and submission. So, close your eyes one more time, breathe in God, and release His peace that already resides within you.

FOLLOW-UP

"My Beloved, Oh how I long for times of intimacy with you – Times that belong to YOU and ME only. Moments where OUR hearts are intertwined as one and MY VOICE, MY HEARTBEAT for you is flowing freely. It's in this place of intimacy that you will fully know how much I desire to be in YOUR presence and how much I love you.

I love you, Papa God."

PROPHETIC WORSHIP & SOAKING

"Nothing Else" – Rick Pino (feat. Abbie Gamboa)

"Abba (Spontaneous Worship)" – Jonathan David Helser

"I Can Hear Your Voice" – Michael W. Smith

"Come Again" – Elevation Worship & Maverick City

DECREES, DECLARATIONS & PROCLAMATIONS

I DECREE, "I AM" who God says "I AM," uniquely and wonderfully made, and my God encounters have been specifically custom-made for me.

I DECLARE, Lord, YOU said in YOUR Word that YOU made me unique and wonderful and YOU custom-made encounters for YOU and me. I stand in full agreement with YOUR Word, "I AM" who YOU said "I AM!"

I PROCLAIM, God created me to be unique, and HE wonderfully made me. "I AM" who HE says "I AM"! I celebrate HIS creation, ME!

JOURNALING

I SPOKE TO YOU BEFORE I FORMED YOU

Thank you, Papa God for sharing your heart with me.
I am so grateful for our special time together.

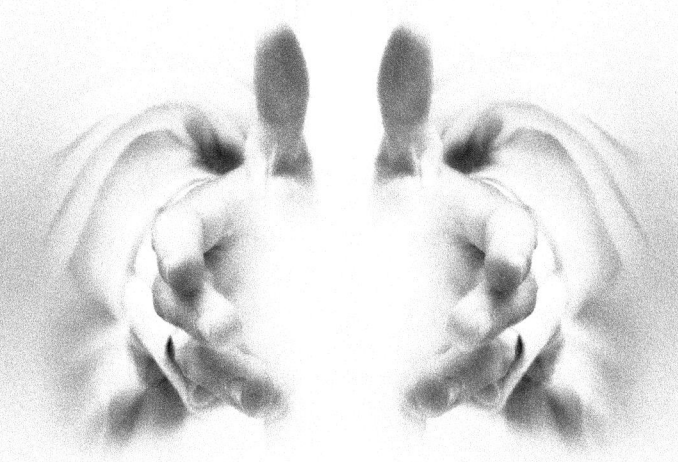

CHAPTER 2

BEFORE YOUR CREATION

QUOTE

"Before God created you, He had already predetermined every unique detail about you, Beloved." – Melissa Hardy

LOVE NOTE

"My Beloved, I am the master Creator, and as your Creator, it is only I who can define you. There is no need to look beyond ME, for I hold the answers to all your questions. Anything or anyone outside of ME will result in a counterfeit response to all your questions relating to your calling, giftings, purpose, identity, and your true authenticity (genuineness, legitimacy, validity, reality, truth, truthfulness, realism). The simplicity in the answers you're searching for simply lie in asking ME this very simple question: 'Papa God, What did YOU say to me before YOU formed me and placed me in my mother's womb?' Ask ME this question, and I will share with you everything I spoke to you before I formed you and

placed you in your mother's womb. It is in MY words that you will discover your true Kingdom Identity – Your Purpose for Life, your Callings and Giftings, and your Authenticity. There are so many things I SPOKE TO YOU, Before Your Time on Earth. Come and hear MY Voice, My Beloved, as I reveal the REAL YOU!

Oh, how I Love you, Papa God."

THE MESSAGE

The very first statement in the Bible reads, *"In the beginning God created..."* (Genesis 1:1, NIV)! Before creation, there was only God, the Father, Son, and Holy Spirit. Take a moment to ponder this question: "What were the Father, Son, and Holy Spirit doing before the creation of the Heavens and the Earth?"

Question Break – Close your eyes and ask Papa God, "Daddy, what were you doing before you created the Heavens and the Earth?"

Journal what you hear Papa God saying to you:

_____

_____

_____

_____

_____

As I asked Papa God this very question, He replied, *"My Beloved daughter, I (WE) were IMAGINING every aspect of the Heavens and the Earth. Every distinctive facet of man, a galaxy and its planets and stars, an ocean and all its living creatures, a jungle with all its plants and animals, and the list goes on and on. Before WE SPOKE CREATION – WE IMAGINED CREATION!"*

Think about how much time God took to imagine everything visible and invisible to mankind. It is beyond your capacity to know and understand the magnitude of God's process of IMAGINATION and His CREATIVE power. You can only comprehend what you can see in the natural, and you have to trust and believe God in the Supernatural. God designed creation this way – there is only one way to unlock the mysteries of creation, and that is through an intimate relationship with Him. It is through this intimacy that you are able to hear His heart and His voice for your life.

Before God CREATED you, He IMAGINED every single thing about you – your purpose, calling, assignments, gifts and talents, and the color of your hair and eyes. God even numbered the hairs of your head: *"Indeed the very hairs of your head are all numbered…"* (Luke 12:7, AMP, alterations mine).

And then GOD SPOKE TO YOU all the things HE had imagined about you – and you responded in agreement – and then He FORMED you and PLACED you in your Mother's womb.

"Before I formed you in the womb I knew you [and approved of you as My chosen instrument], and before you were born I consecrated you [to Myself as My own]…" (Jeremiah 1:5, AMP). In the Book of Psalms, King David wrote, *"For You formed my innermost parts; you*

knit me [together] in my mother's womb. I will give thanks and praise to You, for I am fearfully and wonderfully made; Wonderful are Your works, and my soul knows it very well" (Psalm 139:13-14, AMP).

My Story: I spent 52 years wandering around in the darkness, searching for my identity in all the wrong places. I looked to others for their opinions and validation. I tried to define myself through my career as an Army Soldier. I claimed titles and positions of leadership as my identity – I served in every ministry within the four walls of the church. From day to day, I continued to search and carry the void in my life from year to year, but at the end of each day, I found myself standing in the dark – lost and empty.

But one day, I heard the very words PAPA GOD SPOKE TO ME before HE CREATED ME, and all of a sudden, I found myself standing in the light. There are no words to describe what I experienced in that very moment in time.

ACTIVATION

The Unveiling of Your "God Spoke to You" Moment in Time

The time has come for you to hear the very words GOD SPOKE TO YOU before HE CREATED YOU – He has been waiting on you. Are you ready to hear HIS heart for you, beloved? Simply ask HIM the following question: "Daddy, what did you say to me before you formed me and placed me in my Mother's womb?" Now wait on your Daddy to give you guidance and instructions for your moment in time with Him. Once you've heard from Daddy, it is imperative for you to journal His spoken words.

FOLLOW-UP

Your monumental moment with Papa God is yours alone, and it can be overwhelming, unexplainable, and definitely beyond anything you could ever have imagined. Beloved, you have just returned back to the Father's arms and you're Kingdom Identity – where you belong.

Take all the time you need to bask in His presence and your newly discovered identity. You may find that you need to spend a few days (or longer) quietly meditating on His life-changing words or entering into a time of fasting, prayer, and worship before moving on to the next chapters.

PROPHETIC WORSHIP & SOAKING

"Nothing Else" – Rick Pino (feat. Abbie Gamboa)

"Abba (Spontaneous Worship)" – Jonathan David Helser

"To You" – Maverick City Music and TRIBL (feat. Chandler Moore & Maryanne J. George)

Journey – Maryanne J. George (feat. Mitch Wong)

DECREES, DECLARATIONS & PROCLAMATIONS

I DECREE, God's SPOKEN WORD over me is my true IDENTITY, I was custom-made to fulfill my Kingdom assignment for His Glory, "I AM," who God says "I AM!"

I DECLARE, Father, YOU SPOKE MY TRUE IDENTITY, and YOU custom-made me for YOUR Glory and I walk in my Kingdom Identity. "I AM" who You said "I AM!"

I PROCLAIM, God SPOKE to me before He FORMED me and PLACED me in my Mother's womb, and my identity is sealed in His words – "I AM" who He says "I AM!" I celebrate HIS creation, ME!

JOURNALING

Thank you, Papa God for sharing your heart with me.
I am so grateful for our special time together.

Section II
Called For Such A Time As Now!

"You are my chosen ONE!" – Melissa Hardy

Your Time is Now!

CHAPTER 3

YOU HAVE BEEN CHOSEN

QUOTE

"Beloved, you have been handpicked by God for such a time as this." – Melissa Hardy

LOVE NOTE

"My Beloved, I chose you for such a time as this. You MUST rehear MY Voice – listen to the Words I spoke to you before time – before I formed you and placed you in your Mother's womb. MY WORDS have marked you for MY Glory. MY WORDS have destined you for greatness.

MY WORDS DEFINE YOU!

MY WORDS = YOU!

YOU ARE MY KINGDOM WARRIOR FOR SUCH A TIME AS THIS!

I love you, Papa God."

THE MESSAGE

Right Now! There is a church being birthed out of the womb of the Holy Spirit that has never been seen on Earth before. A church of people who know who they are and who they belong to – a REMNANT OF KINGDOM WARRIORS.

Kingdom Warriors who know and walk in God's truth.

Kingdom Warriors who will supernaturally destroy (abolish, extinguish, and terminate) every plan and plot of the devil and his army.

Kingdom Warriors who will not be moved by the religious ways of man (traditions and doctrines).

Kingdom Warriors who will stand on Godly integrity and righteousness, destroying every selfish, deceiving, and manipulative man-made agenda.

Kingdom Warriors who live from the presence of God and not from a posture of pleasing man.

Kingdom Warriors who know the eternal battle has already been won through the Blood of Jesus Christ and the gates of hell will not prevail.

There is a glory coming out of the REMNANT OF GOD. The finishers have shown up – THAT'S YOU, MY BELOVED. You have been called – "MADE" – for such a time as this!

"God knew what he was doing from the very beginning. He decided from the outset to shape the lives of those who love him along the same lines as the life of his Son. The Son stands first in the line of

humanity he restored. We see the original and intended shape of our lives there in him. After God made that decision of what his children should be like, he followed it up by CALLING people by name. After he CALLED them by name, he set them on a solid basis with himself. And then, after getting them established, he stayed with them to the end, gloriously completing what he had begun." (Romans 8:29-30, MSG, alterations mine)

YOU HAVE BEEN MARKED BY GOD!

Beloved, you have been marked by God to serve in the greatest time in human history. You are HIS Earthly vessel marked to carry out His Kingdom agenda – bringing Heaven to Earth.

> *"Then I looked, and this is what I saw: the Lamb stood [firmly established] on Mount Zion, and with Him a hundred and forty-four thousand who had His name and His Father's name inscribed on their foreheads [signifying God's own possession]."* (Revelation 14:1, AMP)

A seal represented the signet ring used to press wax on official documents, signifying their authenticity, ownership, and protection. However, in Revelation 7:3, the writer is referring to God's servants being sealed with His mark of authenticity and ownership. What a privilege and honor to be chosen and marked by the King of Kings. Beloved, you have been CHOSEN and MARKED!

> *"Saying, 'do not harm the earth nor the sea nor the trees until we seal (mark) the bond-servants of our God on their foreheads.'"* (Revelation 7:3, AMP)

YOU ARE THE LIGHT AND SALT OF THE WORLD

Papa God says, "My Beloved, I have marked you as the salt and light for MY Glory! You are the answers the world is looking for – you carry MY salt and light from Heaven to Earth."

> *"You are the salt of the earth. But if the salt loses its taste, it cannot be made salty again. Salt is useless if it loses its salty taste. It will be thrown out where people will just walk on it. You are the light that shines for the world to see. You are like a city built on a hill that cannot be hidden. People don't hide a lamp under a bowl. They put it on a lampstand. Then the light shines for everyone in the house. In the same way, you should be a light for other people. Live so that they will see the good things you do and praise your Father in heaven."* (Matthew 5:13-16, ERV)

God has called you to be a world influencer! Both salt and light have properties that impact everything around them. Salt heightens flavor and is used as a preservative. Beloved, your calling has been dipped in salt, and it will deliberately (purposefully, intentionally, and calculatingly) influence spheres of people across the Seven Mountains of Society (Family, Religion, Education, Media, Entertainment, Business, and Government). Your salt, the unconditional love of God, shall permeate everywhere it is sprinkled. Light symbolizes your witness concerning the Word of God, and Jesus Christ's journey from the cross to His ascension to Heaven. Jesus gave Himself to redeem you from all wickedness, and He purified you to be Papa God's chosen one. So be eager, zealous, and passionate to do what is beautiful in Papa God's eyes – your calling must have a spiritual impact on the world.

> "He sacrificed himself for us that he might purchase our freedom from every lawless deed and to purify for himself a people who are his very own, passionate to do what is beautiful in his eyes." (Titus 2:14, TPT)

YOU ARE THE VERY ESSENCE OF PAPA GOD'S HEART – "LOVE"

Papa God says, "My Beloved, ask me to give you a deep love for what I have called you to DO – A love that can never be quenched." Beloved, ask Papa God to give you a heart of love for your calling, a love that cannot be quenched (satisfied or extinguished) by anything other than fulfilling your calling. When you walk in love, everything you do will send a sweet-smelling fragrance to Papa God.

> *"…and walk continually in love [that is, value one another – practice empathy and compassion, unselfishly seeking the best for others], just as Christ also loved you and gave Himself up for us, an offering and sacrifice to God [slain for you, so that it became] a sweet fragrance."* (Ephesians 5:2, AMP)

YOU ARE PAPA GOD'S GIFT TO THE WORLD

Papa God says, "My Beloved, flame the fire of the calling that I have placed within you."

Apostle Paul wrote to Timothy, *"I'm writing to encourage you to fan into a flame and rekindle the fire of the spiritual gift God imparted to you when I laid my hands upon you."* (2 Timothy 1:6, TPT)

Beloved, you are God's gift to the world! God desires and requires for you to maintain (preserve, keep up, and sustain) a blazing fire for your calling. Why? Because God has need of you, and the world is waiting for you. God has handpicked specific individuals and assigned them to you and the calling on your life. Ask Papa God to open your ears to hear their cries and to make your heart burn for their healing and deliverance. Never forget you are God's gift to the world for His purpose and glory. The world is waiting – hear their cries!

YOU ARE PAPA GOD'S WARRIOR

Papa God says, "My Beloved, you have been dipped in the Blood of Jesus for warfare, and out of your mouth is a sharp sword. And out of your mouth you shall ROAR MY WORDS, and you shall destroy the enemy and his plans."

Beloved, you have been given the authority to ROAR the very words of God and to destroy (abolish, finish, extinguish, terminate, and put to an end) Satan and his plans. You are a KINGDOM ENFORCER – carrying out what has already BEEN FINISHED ON CALVARY – on the Cross, Descent, Resurrection, and Ascension. The victory has already been won by the Blood of Jesus Christ, and God's Word says you have been dipped in the Blood of Jesus for warfare. So take the Word of God (your authority to ROAR) and the Blood of Jesus (your VICTORY) and join your brothers and sisters – the Remnant of Kingdom Warriors.

> *"And I saw heaven opened, and behold, a white horse, and He who was riding it is called Faithful and True (trustworthy, loyal, incorruptible, steady), and in righteousness He judges and wages*

war [on the rebellious nations]. His eyes are a flame of fire, and on His head are many royal crowns; and He has a name inscribed [on Him] which no one knows or understands except Himself. He is dressed in a robe dipped in blood, and His name is called The Word of God. And the armies of heaven, dressed in fine linen, [dazzling] white and clean, followed Him on white horses. From His mouth comes a sharp sword (His word) with which He may strike down the nations, and He will rule them with a rod of iron; and He will tread the wine press of the fierce wrath of God, the Almighty [in judgment of the rebellious world]. And on His robe and on His thigh He has a name inscribed, 'KING OF KINGS, AND LORD OF LORDS.'" (Revelation 19:11-16, AMP)

CALLED AND PREPARED FOR BATTLE

Kingdom Warriors are battle ready, clothed in the Armor of God: the belt of truth, the breastplate of righteousness, feet fitted with peace, the shield of faith, the helmet of salvation, and the sword of the Spirit, which is the Word of God.

Kingdom Warriors enter the battlefield in confidence and faith, knowing that God is with them and fighting on their behalf.

Kingdom Warriors keep their eyes wide open and their ears and spirit tuned in to the voice of God.

Kingdom Warriors discipline themselves to remain focused – in order to win battles, focus is essential.

Kingdom Warriors maintain a heightened sense of spiritual acuity (divine insight, perception, keenness, sharpness, alertness, and awareness) through prayer.

Kingdom Warriors have faith in prayer to give them strength and help them to persevere in battle.

Kingdom Warriors rely on the Holy Spirit to provide them with strategic wisdom, avenues of protection, and help in remaining surrendered to God's will.

My Story: In 2020, Papa God began to deal with me about The Kingdom Shift taking place on the Earth. As He released prophetic word after prophetic word, I began to see a vision of arms and hands sticking out of the ground – I began to hear them crying for help. As the prophet messages of the End Times began to unfold, I clearly heard Papa God calling me into alignment – into position for such a time as this:

Papa God said, "My Beloved Daughter, I'm coming for My Bride (The Church – My People)… Get Ready! Get Ready! Now is not the time to get relaxed and to be lazy, My people.

Warning, warning, warning, the day is coming soon – Wake Up, Wake Up, Wake Up.

Stop Sleeping! Get off your phones – Turn off your TVs – Stop being distracted by the things of the world. The enemy has lulled you to sleep. My Church is asleep – My Children are asleep – walking around day and night in a trance. Lost in their own selfish ways – self-consumed with their own desires, wants, and needs. They are blinded – their eyes are covered with a veil. Their hands are bound to making money, and their minds are bound by the ways of the world. For you will not be able to withstand the days to come if you remain asleep. The trials and tribulations will swallow you up alive. Many will commit suicide in these times. Many will fall into deep levels of anxiety, stress, and depression. Sickness and illness will overtake their minds and bodies because they are not committed to the true and living vine. They are spiritually dead, malnourished, starving, and anorexic. In the supernatural, they look like the dead bones walking around, so they will find themselves in a pile with other dead bones (like the valley of the dead bones before Me and Ezekiel).

I am calling My Apostles, My Prophets, My Warriors to come forth! Rise Up! Rise Up! Rise Up! And take your places. Pick up your weapons and fight! Go into the Nations, your cities and communities, and assigned territories. Open your mouths and speak to the dead bones – gather what belongs to ME.

Warning, Warning, Warning

Do not be afraid, for you are covered in the Blood of Jesus Christ, surrounded by Warrior Angels and empowered with MY very same power. It is your job to activate, train, develop, and mantle other Apostles and Prophets (the whole fivefold ministry).

Get Up Now! Get Up Now! Move Now! Move Now!

There is no time to wait… If you wait, you will miss the greatest revival of all times. You have everything you need in you, because I placed it in you before the foundations of the world. Before I even thought of every integral aspect of you – Before I Spoke It – Before I breathed life into you – Before I placed you in your Mother's womb. Stop doubting yourself and just know that you know who you are and who you belong to.

Say, I AM WHO I AM – AS JESUS IS, SO AM I!

Now – Open your mouth and say this over and over and over and over. As you speak your identity, you are being branded in the deepest part of your soul. Your soul is not completely aligned with your spirit. Now take dominion of the natural man and force it to align with your spirit and soul. Yes, it will fight, and you will have to manhandle your flesh. Do whatever it takes under the leading of the Holy Spirit.

The days of radical submission are before you. If I call you to a three-day fast, know that I have you and you are covered. You must live a life of submission, fasting, and intercessory prayer. In the days to come, I will download the blueprints for this season and those to come. There is a drastic shift required of My Apostles, My Prophets, and the fivefold ministry. Listen, write it down, and execute in obedience My instructions.

Vision – I see a big warning sign.

I Hear – Warning, Warning, Warning!

I have come to warn you, and I will use you to warn My people, and I will use you to gather My people. I long to crown you in heaven with a crown of jewels and to wrap Myself around you and to speak – Well done, My faithful servant.

Get Up! Get Up! Move Now! Move Now!"

This very prophetic encounter with Papa God changed my life forever. My calling grew arms and legs and I could clearly hear their cries. Everything my husband and I do is connected to fulfilling the calling on our lives for such a time as this. We were made and marked for this era of time in the Kingdom of God!

ACTIVATION

The Shift

Papa God: "My Beloved, the time has come for you to 'Shift' – to realign yourself to what you have already agreed to in Heaven. Remember, 'I Spoke to You' your Kingdom calling before your Creation – and you responded with a 'YES.' And then I formed you (MARKED YOU) and placed you in your Mother's womb and sent you to Earth. I know you are still wondering why I chose you! These conversations you're having with yourself are coming from brokenness. Your brokenness, your past experiences, hurts, failures, and yes, even your sins have nothing to do with ME calling you. For I will use your brokenness in your CALLING for MY Glory. I need for you to realign to your 'YES!' Trust ME, just like you did on your day of creation.

I need for you to close your eyes and listen to MY still voice as 'I SPEAK TO YOU' once again the calling on your life. And when you are ready to give your 'COMPLETE YES,' I need you to let go and take a physical leap forward into MY arms.

It is in MY Arms and in MY Presence – that together WE will walk out your CALLING.

I Love you, Papa God."

FOLLOW-UP

Simply put, you have been chosen for such a time as this for one reason – to BATTLE for the Kingdom of God in this Era. Your calling is connected to the VICTORY that has already been won in Heaven – BEFORE TIME. Beloved, you are merely reliving history! You have already won every battle! You are Papa God's chosen vessel to battle for the advancement of the Kingdom of God. He has already equipped you with everything you need to execute your calling.

"Whatever is, has already been, and whatever will be, already is. God repeats what has passed." (Ecclesiastes 3:15, HCSB)

"You (MY BELOVED) are My battle-axe and weapon of war – for with you I shatter nations, with you I destroy kingdoms." (Jeremiah 51:20, AMP, alterations mine)

PROPHETIC WORSHIP & SOAKING

"Nothing Else" – Rick Pino (feat. Abbie Gamboa)

"Abba (Spontaneous Worship)" – Jonathan David Helser

"Mighty Warrior (Weapon of Warfare)" – Rick Pino

"You're an Army" – Rick Pino

DECREES, DECLARATIONS & PROCLAMATIONS

I DECREE, I am God's battle-axe and weapon of war, I was custom-made to shatter nations and destroy kingdoms, I AM a Kingdom Warrior.

I DECLARE, Father, You call me YOUR BELOVED, and YOU chose me (BEFORE TIME) to be a weapon of mass destruction – I will war on Your behalf, shattering nations and destroying kingdoms.

I PROCLAIM, God SPOKE to me before He FORMED me and PLACED me in my Mother's womb, and HE called me for such a time as this. "I AM" who He says "I AM!" I celebrate HIS creation, A KINGDOM WARRIOR!

JOURNALING

I Spoke to You Before I Formed You

Thank you, Papa God for sharing your heart with me.
I am so grateful for our special time together.

CHAPTER 4

"I AM"

QUOTE

"I am 100% authentic, I am who God says I am, I am His Beloved." – Melissa Hardy

LOVE NOTE

"My Beloved, Be your authentic self, be who I created YOU to be – nothing more and nothing less. For it is in this place of authenticity that YOU will prosper and flourish. It is from your place of authenticity that I will showcase your gifts, your callings, and your true identity. Walk in your Kingdom Authenticity and I will open the Heavens and shine MY flashlight on YOU that all mankind will see Heaven flooding the Earth through YOU and in YOU.

I love you, Papa God."

THE MESSAGE

"Who AM I?" What a great question! People have asked this question for centuries. I'm sure Abraham, Moses, King David, and all our other brothers and sisters in the Bible asked the same question. "Who Am I?" Simply put, the answer is, "As Jesus is, so AM I." So, what does this really mean? It means that YOU are what the Bible says you ARE. God loved you so much that He sent His only Son to Earth to be a living role model for you to follow. Jesus is your role model; therefore, "As Jesus is, so AM I" is not really difficult to figure out. *If God's love is made perfect in us, we can be without fear on the day when God judges the world. We will be without fear, because in this world we are like Jesus"* (1 John 4:17, ERV).

> *Papa God: "My Beloved, everything that you are is capsulated in who my Son is. Because of my deep love for you, I chose to fashion Him into a man and sent Him to Earth to serve as your role model. Why did I do this, you ask? Because of my deep love for YOU and mankind. For you see, it was this great act of love on my behalf, that I created you to be just like MY Son, YOUR Brother. So, just be like My Beloved Son – As Jesus is, so are YOU in this world!"*

WHO AM I?

I AM NEW – As a believer in Christ, I am a new creation. "Therefore if anyone is in Christ [that is, grafted in, joined to Him by faith in Him as Savior], he is a new creature [reborn and renewed by the Holy Spirit]; the old things [the previous moral and spiritual condition] have passed away. Behold, new things have come [because spiritual awakening brings a new life]" (2 Corinthians 5:17, AMP).

I AM FREE – I am free to be who God created me to be. *"Christ has set us free to live a free life. So take your stand! Never again let anyone put a harness of slavery on you"* (Galatians 5:1, MSG)

I AM STRONG – I am strong, and nothing shall overpower me. *"Do not fear [anything], for I am with you; do not be afraid, for I am your God. I will strengthen you, be assured I will help you; I will certainly take hold of you with My righteous right hand [a hand of justice, of power, of victory, of salvation]"* (Isaiah 41:10, AMP).

I AM A LIGHT IN THE DARKNESS – I am the light, the answer to everything the world is in need of. "Jerusalem, get up and shine! Your Light is coming! The Glory of the Lord will shine on you" (Isaiah 60:1, ERV). "This is what the Lord told us to do: 'I have made you a light for the other nations, to show people all over the world the way to be saved'" (Acts 13:47, ERV).

I AM AN OVERCOMER – Through the Blood of Jesus, I have already overcome the trials of this World – I walk in the Victory of the Cross. *"For everyone born of God is victorious and overcomes the world; and this is the victory that has conquered and overcome the world – our [continuing, persistent] faith [in Jesus the Son of God]"* (1 John 5:4, AMP).

I AM A CHILD OF GOD – I am my Father's child, and I have been created in His image. *"And I will be a Father to you, and you will be My sons and daughters,' says the Lord Almighty"* (2 Corinthians 6:18, AMP). *"So God created man in His own image, in the image and likeness of God He created him; male and female He created them"* (Genesis 1:27, AMP).

I AM CHOSEN – I have been chosen for such a time as this. *"You have not chosen Me, but I have chosen you and I have appointed and placed and purposefully planted you, so that you would go and bear fruit and keep on bearing, and that your fruit will remain and be lasting, so that whatever you ask of the Father in My name [as My representative] He may give to you"* (John 15:16, AMP).

I AM RIGHTEOUS – I am righteous not because of who I am in the natural, but because my Daddy lives within me. *"But it is from Him that you are in Christ Jesus, who became to us wisdom from God [revealing His plan of salvation], and righteousness [making us acceptable to God], and sanctification [making us holy and setting us apart for God], and redemption [providing our ransom from the penalty for sin]"* (1 Corinthians 1:30, AMP).

I AM LOVED – I receive God's LOVE, and I freely give it away. *"We love, because He first loved us"* (1 John 4:19, AMP).

I AM AN AMBASSADOR – I am God's sent ambassador to the Nations. *"So we are ambassadors for Christ, as though God were making His appeal through us; we [as Christ's representatives] plead with you on behalf of Christ to be reconciled to God"* (2 Corinthians 5:20, AMP).

I AM REDEEMED – I have been redeemed, and I sit on the throne with my Brother, Jesus – because of the power of The Cross, Descension, Resurrection, and Ascension. *"In Him we have redemption [that is, our deliverance and salvation] through His blood, [which paid the penalty for our sin and resulted in] the forgiveness and complete pardon of our sin, in accordance with the riches of His grace"* (Ephesians 1:7, AMP).

I AM PROTECTED – I am protected by the King of Kings, and I walk under the authority of the Word of God. *"The Lord is my rock, my fortress, and the One who rescues me; My God, my rock and strength in whom I trust and take refuge; My shield, and the horn of my salvation, my high tower – my stronghold"* (Psalm 18:2, AMP).

I AM MORE THAN A CONQUEROR – I have already won every battle. *"I looked, and behold, a white horse [of victory] whose rider carried a bow; and a crown [of victory] was given to him, and he rode forth conquering and to conquer"* (Revelation 6:2, AMP).

I AM PROSPEROUS – I am wealthy in every area of my life, and I have the ability to tap into my storehouse in Heaven at any time. *"Then the Lord your God shall make you abundantly prosperous in everything that you do, in the offspring of your body and in the offspring of your cattle and in the produce of your land; for the Lord will again delight over you for good, just as He delighted over your fathers"* (Deuteronomy 30:9, AMP).

I AM THE TEMPLE OF THE HOLY SPIRIT – I am a holy temple, and the Holy Spirit lives and breathes through me. *"You were bought with a price [you were actually purchased with the precious blood of Jesus and made His own]. So then, honor and glorify God with your body"* (1 Corinthians 6:20, AMP).

I AM ROOTED – I am rooted and grounded in all things God. *"Therefore as you have received Christ Jesus the Lord, walk in [union with] Him [reflecting His character in the things you do and say – living lives that lead others away from sin], having been deeply rooted [in Him] and now being continually built up in Him and [becoming increasingly more] established in your faith, just as you were taught, and overflowing in it with gratitude"* (Colossians 2:6-7, AMP).

My Story: Today, I can stand boldly and state, I am 100% authentic, I am who God says I am, I am His Beloved! After Papa God revealed the very words He "SPOKE TO ME" before He formed me and placed me in my Mother's womb, He continued to emphasize by identity through others. Why? Because He was and is showing off His Beloved (Me) to others... He is letting them know who "I AM IN HIM"... He was and is validating His calling on my life... WHO I AM IN HIM.

Pastors Kenneth and Cynthia Barbour (leaders and mentors) – Papa God said, "You are anointed! There is an apostolic calling on your life. You are a prophet to the church and the Nations (IDENTITY). You need to blaze a trail in what God is calling you to do (INSTRUCTION). You can't get distracted – eagles fly high (WARNING)! There is a great assignment and mandate on your life (ASSIGNMENT). I am getting ready to show you what's to come (ENCOURAGEMENT)."

Evangelist Keshia Freeland (mentor and birthing midwife) – Papa God said, "You are an Eagle Eye prophet (IDENTITY). I called you, don't worry about what man says. Come out of the cave... get up, there is work to do (CORRECTION). There are other prophets waiting on you to put a mantle on them (ASSIGNMENT). I put this in you before I made you. The enemy came and has been trying to kill you, through people and situations, but I have KEPT and PROTECTED you."

During our times of intimacy, Papa God consistently shares His heart about the calling He placed on my life... He is reminding me of our Heavenly conversation before sending me to Earth... He is providing me with guidance and instructions... He is encouraging me to continue to move forward in WHO I AM IN HIM.

Papa God: "My Beloved Daughter, just like my hand was upon your brother Ezekiel, so is it upon you. You will raise up the dead bones. I will send you into the desolate places where My people are crying out to Me for deliverance. I command and appoint you to go forth and to speak to the dry, dead bones...."

Papa God: "My Beloved Daughter, you are draped in My Glory – you are encased in My Glory – My Glory shall flow out of you like a river wide and deep. Ride the waves with Me wherever you go. You are My Fire Warrior, you are My Firebug, you are My Glitter Fire, and you are My Prophet. Before 'I' made you, 'I' saw and spoke FIRE over you. FIRE flows through your whole body – I have branded you with My FIRE."

Be encouraged, Beloved, just be who Papa God created you to be, and He will take care of the rest. It is Papa God's job to shine the spotlight on His Chosen Treasure – YOU!

ACTIVATION

Mirror Reflection

(7-Day Activation)

Question: Who do you see when you look in the mirror? Are your thoughts and images tainted with your own insecurities, self-doubt, low self-esteem, or lack of confidence? Or do you see yourself through God's lenses? This activation is designed to strip away your false (untrue, incorrect, fabricated, made-up, deceitful, and untruthful) images and to replace them with God's images of you.

Over the years, the enemy has been on an assignment to distort your true identity, filling your mind with false self-identity images. This assignment to destroy your true identity began in your early childhood. The enemy used every imaginable tactic and every willing person to sow lies of deceit.

This activation is about uncovering the lies of the enemy and replacing them with God's truths. It is a time of stripping away and uprooting the lies, and a time of healing. Papa God desires for you to free, my beloved.

Through this seven-day process of healing and self-discovery, you will find the freedom and liberty you have been looking for. Activation instructions:

1. Select a time of day when you will not be interrupted and can spend as much time as needed standing before the mirror.

2. Prepare your heart through prayer and worship.

3. Release and surrender yourself to hear from Papa God.

4. Stand before the mirror and say, "Holy Spirit, Holy Spirit, here I am, I release myself in your care, have your way."

5. Listen for Papa God to reveal the lies – this can be painful, BUT Papa GOD is standing right behind you

and watching over you. *"Behold, I am with you and will keep [careful watch over you and guard] you wherever you may go..."* (Genesis 28:15, AMP). So, no matter where this healing process takes you, take comfort in knowing that Papa God is with you.

6. Listen for Papa God to replace the lies with His loving truths about you, beloved.

7. Repeat the process for seven days straight. According to the Bible, the number seven is the number of completeness. We see in the beginning of the Bible that God created the heavens and the earth in six days, and then He rested on the seventh day. He rested because His work had been completed. May you find rest and peace with Papa God on your seventh day.

8. It's important to journal your daily encounters with Papa God.

9. This healing process is a personal time between you and Papa God, and because of the work of the Holy Spirit, it is wise not to share your process or experiences with many people. I would recommend seeking guidance from Papa God in reference to what to share and who to share it with. Papa God may release you to share with your spouse, prayer partner, or someone you can trust to cover you in prayer. The key is not to allow anyone to hinder Papa God's process of healing with their own personal thoughts and desires for you.

My Story: As I spent time before the mirror, Papa God revealed the ugly lies of death and hatred sown by my father. Papa God asked my husband to accompany me to the mirror and to stand behind me as my back protector. He shared with him that he needed to hear the ugliness of my father's hate for me in order to know how to love me from a pure place. It was in this session that I heard my father's audible voice yelling at my mother words of death and hatred for their unborn baby, me.

As the mirror session went on, Papa God continued to reveal the ugliness (violence, cruelty, wickedness, nastiness, and hostility) that was rooted in my father's heart for me as a young child and for my mother. I listened to my father's audible voice yelling horrific things at my mother as he beat her, and in the background, I could hear a little girl crying, me. And then he would direct his anger towards me, shaking me and yelling at me to stop crying. This mirror session went on for 30 minutes as my early childhood was unveiled. Due to the extreme trauma I suffered as a child, I had blocked those memories as a coping mechanism. So, as I stood looking in the mirror, it was as if I was hearing his hatred for the first time; however, I was reliving the trauma all over. As I stood there frozen, unable to move, I could feel the protection of my husband and Papa God.

Papa God used the mirror session to reveal the root cause of the Spirit of an Orphan that I carried for years, which manifested in unworthiness, low self-esteem, power and control tendencies, fear of abandonment, and trust issues. And at the end of the session, Papa God canceled out and replaced the lies of death and hatred with His truth – my identity in Him.

FOLLOW-UP

As you complete these seven days of healing, the Holy Spirit may reveal additional instructions pertaining to your healing process. You may need to seek additional healing through a Christian Counseling Center, a Church Healing Center, reading one or more specific books, or even declaring or decreeing particular scriptures. The Holy Spirit knows the depths of your wounds and the precise healing process just for you! Everyone's healing process is different and unique – it's important not to compare your process with someone else's process. Just take the Holy Spirit's hand and walk out your process of healing. Remember, Papa God desires for you to fully embrace your identity in Him, and this requires you to be healed of the past. When you are whole and healthy, you can now be "AS JESUS IS, SO AM I"! It's from this posture that you will fulfill everything Papa God "SPOKE TO YOU" before He created you.

PROPHETIC WORSHIP & SOAKING

"Nothing Else" – Rick Pino (feat. Abbie Gamboa)

"Abba (Spontaneous Worship)" – Jonathan David Helser

"I Am Your Beloved" – Jonathan David & Melissa Helser, Bethel Music

Who I Am in Christ, Positive Affirmations – I Am Loved by Stephanie McKenna

Who You Say I Am – Hillsong Worship

You Say – Lauren Daigle (Official Music Video)

DECREES, DECLARATIONS & PROCLAMATIONS

Decrees, Declarations, and Proclamations are the most powerful confessions you can say over yourself. They empower you to activate your identity by affirming daily, "AS JESUS IS, SO AM I IN THIS WORLD." Beloved, Papa God desires for you to search His Word and write your own personal "I AM" declarations, decrees, and proclamations. Because of His love for you, His Word is full of His thoughts about you and your identity. A great place to start is with the Book of Ephesians, chapters 1 and 2. An example for you to glean from is provided:

Papa God says, "I Am" His Handiwork.

Scripture Reference: "YOU are Papa God's handiwork, created in Christ Jesus to do good works, which Papa God prepared in advance for YOU to do." (Ephesians 2:6, NIV, alterations mine)

Papa God says, "I Am"

Scripture Reference:

Papa God says, "I Am"

_____

Scripture Reference:

Papa God says, "I Am"

_____

Scripture Reference:

Papa God says, "I Am"

_____

Scripture Reference:

Papa God says, "I Am"

_____

Scripture Reference:

Papa God says, "I Am"

_____

Scripture Reference:

JOURNALING

I SPOKE TO YOU Before I Formed You

Thank you, Papa God for sharing your heart with me.
I am so grateful for our special time together.

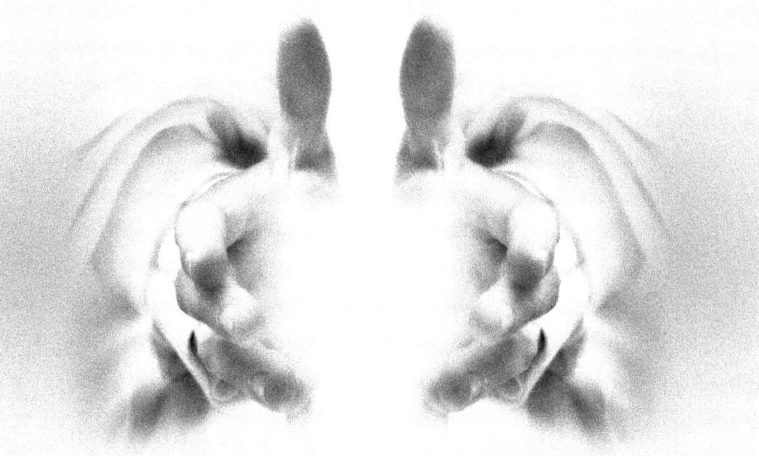

CHAPTER 5

LIVING FROM THE THRONE ROOM

QUOTE

"Beloved, know that you are royalty, take your rightful place in the Throne Room." – Melissa Hardy

LOVE NOTE

"My Beloved, I have already redeemed you from the curse of hell. You died on the cross with MY Beloved Son, Jesus Christ – and you and HE descended to hell and arose on the third day – and now you are seated in heaven on the throne with your Brother, Jesus.

I love you, Papa God."

THE MESSAGE

The Journey to the Throne Room is already done – YOU HAVE ALREADY BEEN REDEEMED! Through THE CROSS, Jesus Christ died for your sins and those of all mankind. The Word of God states that you died on THE CROSS with Jesus. This means you and Jesus DESCENDED to hell and then RESURRECTED on the third day.

> *"For when WE died with Christ WE were set free from the power of sin."* (Romans 6:7, NLT, alterations mine)

> *"...What we believe is this: If we get included in Christ's sin-conquering death, we also get included in his life-saving resurrection.... When Jesus died, he took sin down with him, but alive he brings God down to us.... That's what Jesus did."* (Romans 6:7-11, MSG)

> *"And since we died with Christ, we know we will also live with him. We are sure of this because Christ was raised from the dead, and he will never die again. Death no longer has any power over him. When he died, he died once to break the power of sin. But now that he lives, he lives for the glory of God. So you also should consider yourselves to be dead to the power of sin and alive to God through Christ Jesus."* (Romans 6:8-11, NLT)

After Christ Jesus' resurrection, He focused on the last part of His earthly assignment. He was responsible for COMMISSIONING THE DISCIPLES to fulfill their CALLING; to establish the Kingdom of God (The Church) throughout all nations. And when Christ Jesus finished His assignment, you (through salvation) and He ascended to Heaven and are seated at the right hand of God (His Father).

> *"And HE* (God) *raised US up together with HIM* (CHRIST JESUS) *[when we believed and received Salvation], and seated US with HIM* (GOD) *in the heavenly places, [because we are] in CHRIST JESUS."* (Ephesians 2:6, AMP, alterations mine)

Beloved, when you accepted Jesus Christ as your Lord and Savior, you changed LOCATIONS – from a sinful nature (Earth) to a royal priest (THE THRONE).

> *"But you are a chosen race, a royal priesthood, a consecrated nation, a [special] people for God's own possession, so that you may proclaim the excellencies [the wonderful deeds and virtues and perfections] of Him who called you out of darkness into His marvelous light."* (1 Peter 2:9, AMP)

It is critical for you to understand and live from the power of the finished work – THE CROSS. And living from a finished posture allows you to get into your rightful position and live from a place of victory – THE THRONE. It's time for a paradigm shift: no longer will you view salvation from a conditional posture (an attitude), but from Kingdom posture (a location – THE THRONE). Beloved, are you ready to accept your seat on the throne? Selah!

LIVING FROM THE THRONE ROOM

Beloved, Christ Jesus' sacrifice on THE CROSS wasn't just about redeeming you from your sinful nature and hell. His ultimate mission is to commission and activate the CALLING God placed inside you – the "I SPOKE TO YOU" before I formed you and placed you in your Mother's womb. God's desire for you is to walk out your calling from the Throne Room through HIS POWER AND AUTHORITY.

Everything God has called you to do is already done; all God requires is for you to SIT DOWN and COMMAND earth from HIS THRONE. Beloved, one of the hurdles you will have to overcome is learning how to sit down. You are so used to operating from a posture of performance – physically doing things in the natural, out of your own ability. The devil loves for you to operate from this posture, because he knows:

- ~ You are relying on your own ability to fulfill your calling.
- ~ You are not operating through your Kingdom Power and Authority.
- ~ You have not placed your trust in God.
- ~ You are self-dependent and not God-dependent.

The devil will do everything in his power to keep you from sitting down. Why? Because he knows that if you live from The Throne Room and use your Kingdom Power and Authority, he is defeated. The good news is that the devil has already been defeated and his days on earth are numbered. Hallelujah and Amen!

Beloved, living from "The Throne Room" is your birthright as a son or daughter of God. You have been given the power and authority to:

- Legislate (authorize, establish, decree, and lay down the law) from Heaven to Earth

- Speak (communicate, voice, and declare) from Heaven to Earth

- Command (dictate, order, and direct) from Heaven to Earth

- Rule Earth from Heaven

- Conquer (defeat, overcome, and triumph over) with sweatless Victories

Beloved, Papa God has empowered you to live a victorious life from the Throne Room. Go forth, walk out your calling, and conquer all that has been entrusted to you.

My Story: In May 2022, when my husband and I received the call that one of our family members had attempted suicide, we immediately exercised our throne room authority. At that very moment, we did not know exactly what to pray, so we turned to the Holy Spirit for help and began praying in tongues.

"In the same way the Spirit [comes to us and] helps us in our weakness. We do not know what prayer to offer or how to offer it as we should, but the Spirit Himself [knows our need and at the right time] intercedes on our behalf with sighs and groanings too deep for words." (Romans 8:26, AMP)

We believe that through our partnership with the Holy Spirit, our prayers were legislating (authorizing, establishing, decreeing) and commanding (dictating, ordering, and directing) Heaven to

Earth over our family member. We can only imagine what the Holy Spirit was decreeing and declaring in the heavens.

_____'s identity is firmly rooted and established in Christ's love. _____ has grasped how wide and long and high and deep Papa God's love is for them.

_____ knows that Papa God will never forget or neglect them. _____ knows that their name is engraved on the palms of Papa God's hands.

_____ has turned back from the pit of hell, and the light of life shines on them.

_____ belongs to you, Papa God. And they rest in your presence, safe from the condemnation of their own heart.

As we continued to pray in tongues, we also began to decree that our family member would live – over and over. And as we decreed life, Papa God spoke and said, "All is well, and they shall live and fulfill their calling." The peace of God within us bubbled up, and we began to worship Papa God for the victory for our family member.

As we have cultivated our relationship with Papa God, we have found it easier to live from His Throne Room in all situations. It was because of our relationship with Papa God (our encounters) that we were able to handle this situation from the Throne Room. We believe every Papa God encounter prepares you for what is to come… for the next level in Him.

ACTIVATION

Sitting in "The Throne Room"

(3-Day Activation)

Through a three-day process, seek Papa God and ask Him to reveal "HIS THRONE ROOM" to you. Activation instructions:

1. Select a time of day when you will not be interrupted and can spend as much time as needed sitting in God's presence.

2. Prepare your heart through prayer and worship.

3. Release and surrender yourself to Papa God.

4. Close your eyes and see yourself sitting in The Throne Room.

    - What does it look like?

    - What does it feel like?

    - What does it smell like?

    - What is Papa God saying to you?

5. Make sure to journal your Throne Room encounters.

FOLLOW-UP

Beloved, your journey to the Throne Room has already been purchased by Christ Jesus. You are seated with the Son of God, Christ Jesus, at the right hand of God in Heaven.

"And HE (God) raised US up together with HIM (CHRIST JESUS) [when we believed and received Salvation], and seated US with HIM (GOD) in the heavenly places, [because we are] in CHRIST JESUS" (Ephesians 2:6, AMP, alterations mine)

You have been given the power and authority to legislate, command, and speak Heaven to Earth. God has entrusted you to rule Earth from Heaven and granted you the ability to walk in sweatless victories. Go forth and do what you are famous for in Heaven – YOUR CALLING!

PROPHETIC WORSHIP & SOAKING

"Nothing Else" – Rick Pino (feat. Abbie Gamboa)

"Abba (Spontaneous Worship")" – Jonathan David Helser

"Yours (Glory and Praise)" – Elevation Worship (live, 2017)

Throne Room Song – Charity Gayle (feat. Ryan Kennedy) (Live)

I Speak Jesus – Charity Gayle

Hydrated Soaking Music – Steve Swanson

DECREES, DECLARATIONS & PROCLAMATIONS

I DECREE, I am God's beautiful crown of glory and splendor, a royal crown in HIS hand for all to see.

I DECLARE, Father, YOU have called me a crown of glory and splendor, and YOU chose me to be of royal descent – a royal crown in YOUR hands for the world to see and marvel.

I PROCLAIM, God SPOKE to me, "You will be like a beautiful crown that the LORD holds up, a royal crown, exceedingly beautiful, in MY hands."

JOURNALING

I SPOKE TO YOU Before I Formed You

Thank you, Papa God for sharing your heart with me.
I am so grateful for our special time together.

Section III
A Time Of Healing

"For the Blood of Jesus Christ has made you WHOLE!" – Melissa Hardy

You have been healed through the LOVE of GOD

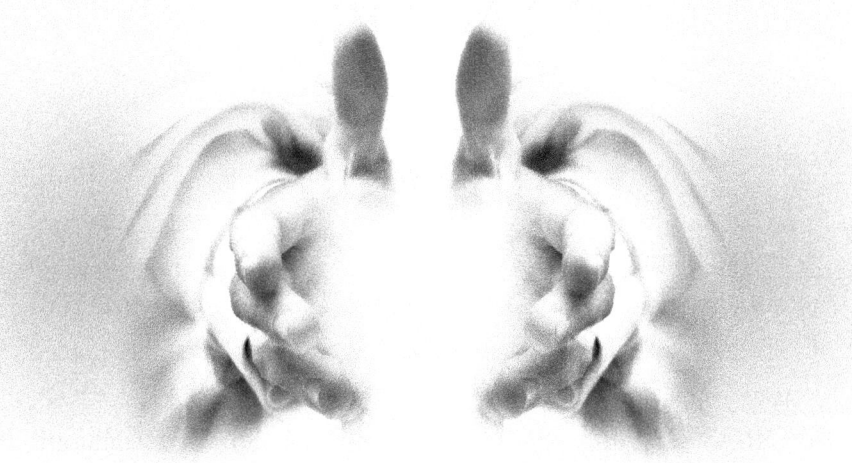

CHAPTER 6

STRONGHOLDS

QUOTE

"You have already won the battle – AS JESUS IS, SO ARE YOU!" – Melissa Hardy

LOVE NOTE

"My Beloved, When I created you, you were PERFECT – then you entered a sinful world – and through MY SON, you have been redeemed (through the CROSS, BLOOD, and SALVATION) to your original state of PERFECTION. It is through the healing process of stripping away the tactics and plans of the devil that you – MY BELOVED – will walk in total FREEDOM, which was purchased by the BLOOD OF CHRIST JESUS.

I love you, Papa God."

THE MESSAGE

Beloved, from the moment you were born, the devil has desired to kill you and abort the calling on your life. The very words Papa God "SPOKE TO YOU" before He formed you and placed you in your Mother's womb – yes, those WORDS, HIS VERY WORDS TO YOU – have been the motive behind every demonic assignment to destroy you, BELOVED. While the battle to destroy you (to do away with you) has been fierce (brutal), the devil does not have the authority to kill you – unless you give it to him. Remember the words of your brother, Christ Jesus.

> *"For this reason the Father loves ME (Christ Jesus), because I lay down MY [own] life so that I may take it back. No one takes it away from ME, but I lay it down voluntarily. I am authorized and have power to lay it down and to give it up, and I am authorized and have power to take it back. This command I have received from My Father."* (John 10:17-18, AMP, alterations mine)

You have the same POWER and AUTHORITY to defeat the devil and to fulfill your calling in victory. AS JESUS IS, SO ARE YOU!

THE DEMONIC ATTACK

The devil has mastered the ability to attack you through lies (untruths), unforgiveness, and bondage through demonic activity. This chapter will UNCOVER (expose and reveal) these three tactics. Kindly note, the devil has an arsenal of tactics; therefore, it is highly recommended that you spend time with Papa God seeking specific revelation pertaining to your healing needs.

DEMONIC LIES (UNTRUTHS) – The devil uses others and himself to sow lies in your life to attack your self-identity ("stupid, ugly, fat," etc.) These lies are the root of low self-esteem, unworthiness, promiscuity, sexual orientation, LGBT (Lesbian, Gay, Bisexual, Transgender) and other communities, trying to please people, control issues, and perfectionism (to name a few).

UNFORGIVENESS – The devil uses unforgiveness of others and self to hold you hostage in offense, anger, bitterness, shame, depression, anxiety, stress-induced medical conditions, sleep deprivation, Post-Traumatic Stress Disorder (PTSD), cutting, and suicide (to name a few). Sometimes it's easier to forgive others, while still holding yourself captive in the prison of unforgiveness. Unforgiveness of self is not just about not forgiving yourself, but about holding yourself responsible for others' actions – for example, "If I didn't drink at the party, he/she would not have raped me." Unforgiveness can be rooted in abuse (mental, emotional, and physical), rape, abortions, and molestation (to name a few).

Beloved, if you've thought about harming yourself or believe life is hopeless:

Please take a deep breath – Hold It – and RELEASE…

Take another deep breath – Hold It – and RELEASE…

And take one more deep breath – Hold it – and RELEASE.

And repeat these words over and over – I WILL LIVE and not die! I WILL LIVE and not die! I WILL LIVE and not die!

Surrender everything you have been carrying to Papa God and place your trust in HIM, and seek immediate help from a pastor, family member, friend, co-worker, or suicide prevention organization.

If you reside in the United States, contact the National Suicide Prevention Lifeline (1-800-273-8255), 911, or 988; in other countries, contact your local emergency number. Suicide organizations provide 24-hour free and confidential support for people in distress, along with prevention and crisis resources.

"Casting all your cares [all your anxieties, all your worries, and all your concerns, once and for all] on Him, for He cares about you [with deepest affection, and watches over you very carefully]." (1 Peter 5:7, AMP)

BONDAGE – The devil and his servants have placed people in bondage through exposure to demonic activity – portals (open doors) to the Demonic Realm. These realms include mediums, psychics, fortune-tellers, tarot card readings, séances, horoscopes, paranormal phenomena, talking to the dead, seeking after ghosts, playing with Ouija boards, watching horror movies or television shows, listening to music with explicit lyrics (profanity, murder, and suicide), pornography, masturbation, and secret societies (to name a few).

The devil has embedded himself throughout your community – doing his work in plain sight. He can be found in secret societies (temples, shrines, buildings), botanicas (witchcraft shops/stores), liquor stores, nightclubs, and sex shops (to name a few). The devil has even invaded your television, radio stations, and cell phone through social media and advertisements. Exposure to the demonic realm can lead to mental illnesses (bipolar disorder, schizophrenia, and obsessive compulsive disorder), murder, and abusive behavior (to name a few).

The devil in his craftiness desires to trap you in his lies and trickery. One of the tricks of the devil is to make you believe he doesn't exist. You may be bound by the devil and not even realize it. Society has normalized the schemes of the devil and has attacked the righteousness of God.

Beloved, you have two doors in your life: one is your mind and the other is your heart. These two doors are the gateways to your soul. Papa God and the devil are battling daily for access to your soul (your mind and heart). Papa God so longs to control the access to your heart and mind.

> *"Here I am! I stand at the door and knock. If you hear my voice and open the door, I will come in and eat with you. And you will eat with me."* (Revelation 3:20, ERV)

Beloved, who owns the doors to your mind and heart? Take a moment to reflect on this question and be truthful with yourself.

_____

_____

ACTIVATION

Identifying the Tactics of the Devil

(7-Day Activation)

Through this seven-day process, seek Papa God and ask Him to identify the tactics of the devil pertaining to your life and calling. Activation instructions:

1. Select a time of day when you will not be interrupted and can spend as much time as needed in the presence of Papa God.

2. Daily prepare your heart through prayer, worship, and the Word of God, through the leading of the Holy Spirit.

3. Release and surrender yourself to Papa God. The key to healing is being honest and vulnerable with Papa God.

4. Ask Papa God these questions and write His responses in your healing journal.

    Demonic Lies

    What lies have been sown in your life?

    Unforgiveness

    Are there people in your life that you have not forgiven?

    Are you holding yourself in the prison of unforgiveness?

    If so, why, and what happened?

    Are you experiencing any conditions associated with unforgiveness?

Bondage

Have you engaged in demonic activity?

Beloved, if you have engaged in demonic activity (knowingly or unknowingly), there is no condemnation or shame. Adam and Eve were perfect and communed with Papa God daily, and they were tricked by the devil. God loves you so much, He desires to free you from the chains of bondage.

5. Kindly, do not continue to read "I SPOKE TO YOU" until you complete your seven-day activation.

FOLLOW-UP

Beloved, in order to begin the healing process, it was critical for you and Papa God to expose the demonic attack(s) on your life and calling. You have now discovered the root causes of your physical, mental, and emotional issues. In chapter 7, you and Papa God will enter into the operating room, a place of deep healing and restoration.

PROPHETIC WORSHIP & SOAKING

"Nothing Else" – Rick Pino (feat. Abbie Gamboa)

"Abba (Spontaneous Worship)" – Jonathan David Helser

The Altar Sessions (Live Volume 1) – Rick Pino

"You Restore Everything" – Rick Pino (feat. Abbie Gamboa)

"I Speak Jesus" – Charity Gayle (feat. Steven Musso)

"He Knows My Name" – Francesca Battistelli (Official Music Video)

"I Can't Get Away" & "Downpour" – Melissa Helser (feat. Naomi Raine), live

"Sound Mind" & "Turning On the Lights" – Melissa Helser

DECREES, DECLARATIONS & PROCLAMATIONS

I DECREE, I am your Beloved, and yet in all these things I am more than a conqueror and I have the victory through Jesus Christ, who died on the cross for me.

I DECLARE, Father, I am more than a conqueror through Jesus Christ, and by the Blood of Jesus Christ I walk in total victory! I have already defeated the attacks of the devil! I WIN!

I PROCLAIM, Papa God's Word tells me, amidst all these attacks I am more than a conqueror and I have the victory through my Brother Jesus Christ because of His love for me.

JOURNALING

_____

_____

_____

_____

_____

_____

_____

_____

_____

_____

_____

_____

_____

_____

Thank you, Papa God for sharing your heart with me.
I am so grateful for our special time together.

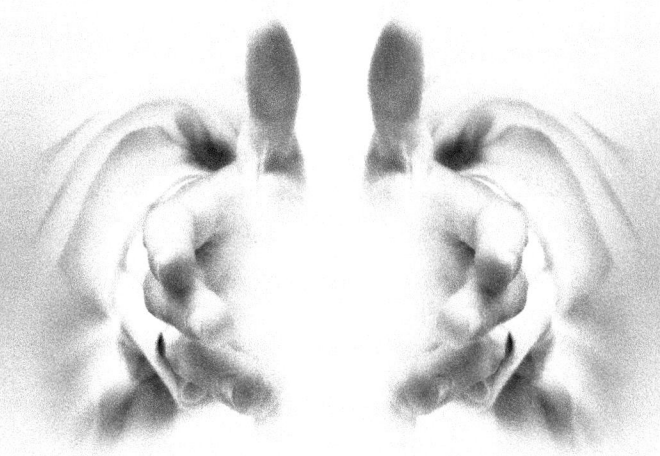

CHAPTER 7

A Choice To Heal

QUOTE

"I AM YOUR FATHER, the healer
you have been searching for…

I AM YOUR FATHER, the ONE who created
you and the ONE who will heal you…

I AM YOUR FATHER, I will turn your
pain into beauty for MY GLORY."

– Melissa Hardy

LOVE NOTE

*"My Beloved, I know the condition of your heart – I know
the deep things, those you don't even remember – I am the
SURGEON OF YOUR HEART. I have come to place you on*

MY SURGICAL TABLE. The time has come to do a deep healing of your heart. Come and take MY HAND and enter into the OPERATING ROOM, and let the healing process begin.

I love you, Papa God."

THE MESSAGE

Beloved, throughout "I SPOKE TO YOU," I have chosen to share pieces of my story of healing. I pray my story will minister to you and you will find the courage to walk out your own healing story.

My Story – My Healing Journey (Operating Room) began in my late 30s and has spanned over 20 years. Due to the depth of the trauma, Papa God healed me layer by layer – operation after operation. It's like He was peeling an onion – one layer at a time. As Papa God peeled a layer, He knew how far to go, and He always allowed for the wound to heal completely before going to the next layer. At times, Papa God would wait months or even a year before peeling the next layer. Why? Because He knew exactly the right timing for the next level of healing.

Over the years, Papa God used various surgical procedures (methods) and different people (operating staff) to assist with the healing process. Early in the process, He sent me to Genesis Christian Counseling Center to heal from the molestation, sexual harassment, and abuse. Next, He sent me to:

~ Kingdom Bible Institute – to heal my heart and build a biblical foundation

- ~ Victory Bible College – to deal with my trust issues, develop the Fruit of the Spirit, and build a strong supernatural biblical foundation

- ~ Eagles International Training Institute – to prepare and activate the calling on my life

I am truly grateful for Papa God and those who have ministered healing to me over the years. As I look back over the years, a large amount of my healing took place one on one – just me and Papa God.

I remember one day, Papa God said to me, "Daughter, I want to take you into the healing pool. I have shared with you before that the Spirit of Infirmity has attacked you for years and years. The devil has used the Spirit of Infirmity to try to kill your calling – to keep you off focus – and to cut your life short; however, it will flee because of My healing power. Trust Me, daughter, I am calling you into the pool – take one step at a time and submerge yourself into the pool!" As I submerged myself in the pool, Papa God began to heal various areas of my body.

When He finished the healing session, He began to speak again: "The devil has attacked your body with a vengeance because you are a Healer to the Nations, just as you are a Prophet to the Nations. You shall heal large groups of people without even touching them. For My healing power will be released through you – as you walk by people, they will be healed through your shadow. Why? Because My healing power will just ooze out of you."

The one thing that hindered my healing early on was not completely trusting Papa God through the process. I had to learn how to receive His love in order to trust Him with my heart and my deep wounds.

Another area that hindered my healing process was my lack of faith. I had to grow faith – and believe – in Papa God's healing power in order to open the door for His healing power to flow in my life.

Beloved, as you enter into the Operating Room, know that Papa God is a gentleman: He will never conduct a surgery without your surrendered "yes." As you enter into the healing process, I pray you will offer up a surrendered "yes" to Papa God daily.

ACTIVATION

Operating Room

(30-Day Activation)

The time has come to uproot (evacuate, deracinate, pull up, and dig up) the lies, tricks, and plans of the devil. Papa God is calling you into the operating room for 30 days. During this time of deep healing and stripping away, the lies will be replaced with Papa God's truth, and your chains of bondage and unforgiveness will be broken. Papa God knows all your secrets and the depth of your battle wounds. Activation instructions:

1. Select a time of day when you will not be interrupted and can spend as much time as needed in the operating room with Papa God.

2. Daily prepare your heart through prayer, worship, and the Word of God, through the leading of the Holy Spirit.

3. Release and surrender yourself to Papa God. The key to healing is being honest and vulnerable with Papa God.

4. Daily ask Papa God these questions and journal His responses and your healing journey.

   - Ask Papa God, "What do you want to operate on today?" Sometimes Papa God will stay in one area for a few days – just follow His lead.

   - Ask yourself, "Why am I dealing with this?" Be vulnerable and honest with yourself and Papa God can be painful. Be encouraged, freedom awaits you on the other side.

   - Ask Papa God, "Why am I dealing with this?" Be open to hear His heart and voice!

   - Ask Papa God, "What can I do today and moving forward to improve in this area?" Be open to receive His correction and instructions. He may require you to fast for a certain time period with specific instructions; read a particular scripture or listen to a certain song; or even speak with your pastor.

5. Through your 30-day healing process, Papa God may reveal areas in your life requiring in-depth Christian counseling. Papa God knows your healing process from the beginning to the end; He is the Alpha "the beginning"

and the Omega "the end." Beloved, surrender and trust Papa God and His process of healing for you.

6. Kindly, do not continue to read "I SPOKE TO YOU" until you complete your 30-day healing activation.

FOLLOW-UP

"My Beloved,

Oh, how I have delighted and enjoyed our time together in the operating room...

Healing you has brought Me such pleasure...

My living waters have flown freely throughout your heart, mind, and physical body...

I have restored you back to your unique state of perfection through the Blood of Jesus Christ...

I will use your life as a beacon of light for the world to see My Glory...

You will heal, deliver, and set others free through your story of healing and deliverance...

While the devil planned to kill the very words 'I SPOKE TO YOU'...

he was defeated before 'I EVEN SPOKE TO YOU'...

You see, My Beloved, what 'I SPOKE TO YOU' before I formed you and placed you in your Mother's womb...

Is My very presence inside of you, for My Glory...

So arise, My Beloved, I HAVE MADE YOU WHOLE, and YOU ARE FREE!

I love you, Papa God."

PROPHETIC WORSHIP & SOAKING

"Nothing Else" – Rick Pino (feat. Abbie Gamboa)

"Abba (Spontaneous Worship)" – Jonathan David Helser

The Altar Sessions (Live Volume 1) – Rick Pino

"Learning to Be Loved by You" – Melissa Helser

"I Am Your Beloved" & "Running Home" – The Helser's

"New Wine" – Maverick City Music

When I Lock Eyes with You" – Maverick City Music

"The One You Love" – Maverick City and Kirk Franklin

Echo In Jesus Name – Charity Gayle (Live)

DECREES, DECLARATIONS & PROCLAMATIONS

I DECREE, I am your Beloved, and Your living waters have healed my heart, mind, and physical body. I am a living testimony for the world to see.

I DECLARE, Father, You are my HEALER, and Your Rivers of living water flow throughout my heart, mind, and physical body. By the Blood of Jesus Christ I am healed! I am delivered! I am set free!

I PROCLAIM, Papa God SPOKE to me, "Beloved, you are healed, delivered, and set free, and I have restored you back to your unique state of perfection through the Blood of Jesus Christ."

JOURNALING

Thank you, Papa God for sharing your heart with me.
I am so grateful for our special time together.

Section IV
Cultivating Your Relationship With God

"Cultivating your Calling is Relational – it is the intimacy between you and Papa God." – Melissa Hardy

Relationship is the Key to Papa God's Heart

CHAPTER 8

THROUGH DYING TO SELF

QUOTE

"Cultivation is a fluid, ongoing process and is never-ending." – Melissa Hardy

LOVE NOTE

"My Beloved, Cultivating is really about the time you spend in MY presence, through reading My Word and communing with ME in prayer and in worship. For only I can truly cultivate what I have placed inside you for the Kingdom and for MY Glory. This is because only I, your CREATOR, truly know what you need to grow and bloom into the very words 'I SPOKE TO YOU' before I created you and placed you in your Mother's womb and sent you to Earth. In and through your relationship with ME, I will use others in your development process. Why? Because they too belong to ME and I will use them in your life as I see fit. I will also place other requirements on you based on the calling on your life.

Your instructions will not look like those of others – for your set of instructions has been uniquely designed just for you. No matter the process, the How, What, When, and Where, all you have to do is remember it is ME orchestrating your seasons of cultivation. Stay planted like a tree by the water and connected to the vine – for I AM your living water and I AM the gardener of your life.

I love you, Papa God."

(John 15:1, 5, NIV; Jeremiah 17:8, NIV)

Seasons of cultivation are fluid, ongoing processes – they are never-ending. Why? Because your Father is always moving – He is always doing a new thing. Therefore, He is always doing a new thing in you and through you – these are the seasons of your life. You preparation time is not just a season, it's seasons – as you serve Papa God from season to season, you will also go from glory to glory with Him.

It's important to embrace your seasons of cultivation and understand that you will never arrive at the finish line of cultivation (preparation) during your time on Earth. When you cross over into Heaven and you hear "Well done, good and faithful servant…" (Matthew 25:23, NIV), then you have crossed the finish line of cultivating your Earthly relationship with your Father.

THE MESSAGE

Beloved, you cannot be sent to a community, to a group of people, or to a Nation without the process of cultivation (preparation). Papa God's SPOKEN WORDS TO YOU require seasons of cultivation, a process of maturing. Cultivation is really about growing in your relationship with Papa God. As you go deeper in your relationship with Papa God, it's from this place that He prepares you, your gifting's, talents, and callings for the next season of assignment(s). Every new season of ministry will require a pre-season of cultivation.

CULTIVATING YOUR RELATIONSHIP WITH PAPA GOD BY DYING TO SELF

Cultivating a relationship with Papa God involves seasons of dying to self and becoming more like your Father. You must choose to hold your Soul (Mind, Emotions, and Free Will) and your Fleshly Man under subjection to your Spirit Man.

> Spirit – Your Spirit comes alive when you accept Jesus Christ as your LORD and Savior. This is how you communicate, interact, and commune with Papa God.

> Soul – Your Mind (your thoughts), Emotions (your feelings), and your Free Will (your choices). The soul has the tendency to be self-centered, self-consumed, and just plain selfish.

> **Note: many see the Spirit and the Soul as one and the same; however, scripture clearly separates the two through function. *"God's word is alive and working. It is sharper than the sharpest sword and cuts all the way into us. It cuts deep to the place where the soul and the spirit are joined. God's word cuts to the center of our joints and our bones. It judges the thoughts and feelings in our hearts"* (Hebrews 4:12, ERV).

> Fleshly Man – Your senses (sight, hearing, smell, taste, and touch), are the easiest aspects of your creation to understand.

This is because your senses are tangible (physical, real, noticeable, touchable, concrete, and perceptible). Just because the fleshly man is listed last doesn't make him less important. God created your natural man to house your Senses, Soul, and Spirit man, and it is the vessel He uses to execute Heaven on Earth. *"You should know that your body is a temple for the Holy Spirit that you received from God and that lives in you. You don't own yourselves. God paid a very high price to make you his. So honor Papa God with your body"* (1 Corinthians 6:19-20, ERV.)

Papa God desires for you to live by the Spirit and not according to your Soul or your Fleshly man. He is calling you to live a life that glorifies HIM in all that you do. To do this, you must die to your fleshly desires (selfishness, sin), pick up your cross (your problems, imperfections, and weaknesses), and daily yield to your Spirit. Through salvation you are a new creature in your spirit.

"Therefore if anyone is in Christ [that is, grafted in, joined to Him by faith in Him as Savior], he is a new creature [reborn and renewed by the Holy Spirit]; the old things [the previous moral and spiritual condition] have passed away. Behold, new things have come [because spiritual awakening brings a new life]" (2 Corinthians 5:17, AMP).

And you must retrain your mind to think as a new creation before you're able to manifest the perfect will of God in your flesh. *"So I beg you, brothers and sisters, because of the great mercy God has shown us, offer your lives as a living sacrifice to him – an offering that is only for God and pleasing to him. Considering what he has done, it is only right that you should worship him in this way. Don't change yourselves to be like the people of this world, but let God change you inside with a new way of thinking. Then you will be able to understand and accept what God wants for you. You will be able to know what is good and pleasing to him and what is perfect"* (Romans 12:1-2, ERV). As you continually transform your natural man into your spiritual man, your relationship with the Father will continue to blossom.

> *My Story - For me personally, dying to self is an ongoing process which requires me to surrender (to submit, yield, and lay down my life) to Papa God daily. It is through this process of surrendering my life that I am able to die daily to my own fleshly desires and become more like Papa God. Dying to self requires me to stay focused on "HIM and HIS WILL and DESIRES" and not "MY WILL and DESIRES." What does that look like for me?*
>
> ~ *First, having the right relationship priorities – Papa God is always first, followed by my husband, my children, and my immediate family. Next, is relationships with others (friends, co-workers) and my service to the Kingdom of God.*
>
> ~ *Second, I am intentional in cultivating my relationship with Papa God. I purposefully plan to spend time with My Papa God daily through prayer, worship, reading His Word, conversation, and gratitude:*
>
> ○ *We spend time first thing in the morning.*
>
> ○ *I look for opportunities throughout the day to interact with Him.*
>
> ○ *And we spend time together before I close my eyes to enter into peaceful sleep.*

- ~ *Thirdly, I surrender my will to Papa God and posture myself to do His Will for the day.*
  - *I purposefully look for opportunities to share Papa God's love with others through kind acts.*
  - *I purposefully look for opportunities to share Papa God's wisdom through words of knowledge.*
  - *I purposefully look for opportunities to walk in the Fruit of the Spirit, like being patient with others.*

I truly believe that when Papa God sees my willingness to become more like Him through dying to self, He is experiencing the depth of my love for Him.

ACTIVATION

"Taking Your Cross to the Throne Room"

(Seven-Day Activation)

Papa God wants for you to pick up your cross (for example, fleshly desires, problems, imperfections, weaknesses) and bring them to Him in the Throne Room.

Activation Instructions:

1. Listen to the worship song "Abba" by Jonathan David Helser.

2. Spend 20 to 30 minutes in His presence (no music, no cell phone, and no distractions).

3. Share your heart (your cross) with Papa God.

4. Sit quietly in His presence, allowing Papa God to do His work.

5. Make sure to journal your Papa God encounters.

You throne room experiences may include an outpouring of Papa God's love, healing, correction, or even instruction. Remain open to just receive from Papa God, trusting that He knows exactly what you need during your intimate moments with Him.

FOLLOW-UP

Remember, it is extremely critical for you to embrace your seasons of cultivation and understand that you will never arrive at the finish line of cultivation (preparation) during your time on Earth. Dying to self is one of the ways you allow Papa God to prepare you for ministry. Papa God's "SPOKEN WORDS TO YOU" require you to pick up your cross and to die to self in order to fulfill your Kingdom Calling. My Beloved, it is through your willingness to be cultivated that Papa God is preparing you to be sent to a community, to a group of people, or to a Nation.

PROPHETIC WORSHIP & SOAKING

"Nothing Else" – Rick Pino (feat. Abbie Gamboa)

"Abba (Spontaneous Worship)" – Jonathan David Helser

"Yeshua" – Jesus Image and Michael Koulianos

We Fall Down – Jenn Johnson

I Surrender – Hillsong (feat. Lauren Daigle)

DECREES, DECLARATIONS & PROCLAMATIONS

I DECREE my old self was nailed to the cross with my brother Jesus, my sins were done away with, and I am no longer a slave to sin.

I DECLARE in prayer, "Lord, You said in Your Word that my old man was nailed to the cross with my brother Jesus. I stand in full agreement that my sins were canceled out by the blood of Jesus and I am no longer a slave to sin."

I PROCLAIM that I died on the cross with Jesus and all my sins have been canceled out by the blood of Jesus, and I am no longer bound in slavery to sin.

JOURNALING

Thank you, Papa God for sharing your heart with me.
I am so grateful for our special time together.

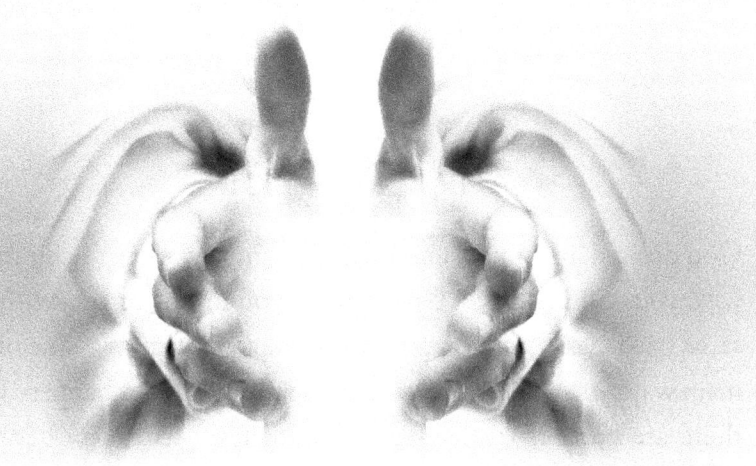

CHAPTER 9

Through Intimacy

QUOTE

"Intimacy is the key to Papa God's heart." – Melissa Hardy

LOVE NOTE

"My Beloved, My heart aches to be intertwined with your heart. 'I WANT' to hear you whisper how much you love ME and only ME. 'I WANT' to be the center of your attention and in your every thought. 'I WANT' for you to delight in ME and the things of MY Kingdom. 'I WANT' for your eyes to be focused on MY splendor and beauty. 'I WANT' for your sweet lips to sing worship to ME day and night. 'I WANT' for you to crawl up into my arms and allow ME to stroke your hair. 'I WANT' to feel your breath on MY face. 'I WANT, I WANT, I WANT' everything about you to ache for ME and ME alone.

I love you, Papa God."

THE MESSAGE

God desired, imagined, and created intimacy solely to commune with you. God is Love! God created you in His image, with the same need, desire, and capacity for intimacy. Intimacy is one of the main ways you are just like your Father. Love cannot happen when there are barriers (walls, fences, obstacles, barricades) between you and God, or between you and others. That is why the ONE GOD – the Father, Son, and Holy Spirit – are intertwined in love as ONE.

Think about why God came to Earth in the person of Jesus: He came to remove the barriers between you and Himself. That is why God created you for intimacy. No person, even in the healthiest of relationships, can meet your need for TRUE ENDLESS INTIMACY (boundless, infinite, limitless, never-ending, and ceaseless). Only your Creator – Your Father – can meet your deepest needs for intimacy.

You can pursue intimacy with your Father through reading and studying the Word of God, intercessory prayer, fasting and consecration, worship, and living a life of obedience and submission out of your love for Him. While all of these interactions create an atmosphere of intimacy, the Father is simply looking for you to crawl up in his lap and gaze passionately into His eyes. For your eyes are the windows to your HEART and LOVE for Him.

> *My Story: For years, I could never understand or comprehend when people would refer to God as their Father or Daddy, even after I accepted Jesus Christ as my Lord and Savior. I would hear them make such loving comments in reference to their intimate moments with their Father or Daddy. I would think to myself,*

"Who are they talking about? God is the person who will punish me when I make a mistake or sin." My view of God had been tainted by the lies and plans of the devil. My view of God was based on my relationship with my natural father:

My father who disciplined in sternness (severity and harshness) – with an iron fist.

My father who expected perfection and did not allow for anything less – no room for mistakes.

My father who never displayed emotions of love – no "I love you" – no hugs – no laughter.

My father who communicated through hurtful words – no loving conversation – no words of affirmation.

My father who physically, emotionally, and verbally abused his family – rooted in his own childhood abuse.

Beloved, the devil hates Godly relationships, and he knows your personal relationships with your natural father, mother, and others are directly connected to your relationship with your heavenly Father (natural father), Jesus Christ (siblings and friends), and the Holy Spirit (mother). This is why he works really hard to destroy your relationships at a very young age. While attending Bible College, I went through a healing process pertaining to my relationship with my natural father, mother, and others. Through this process, the lies and tricks of the devil were exposed, and I was able to release and forgive my natural father and mother, among many others. It was through this process that I was able to see God as My Papa God – as My Father – as My Daddy.

You know, the one where you can climb up in His lap and He tells you everything will be all right.

The one who will hug you and shower you with love.

The one who will dry your tears and comfort you.

The one who will never hurt or harm you.

Beloved, I encourage you to dig deep into this chapter's activations, allowing Papa God to reveal the lies and tricks the devil has sown in your life. The ones that are designed to destroy your calling – the very words Papa God "SPOKE TO YOU." As you heal your natural relationships, you will see your relationship with Papa God, Jesus Christ, and the Holy Spirit blossom. You will experience the very essence of Papa God's love for you – a relationship of intimacy – just as I have."

ACTIVATION 1

Healing the Wound of a Natural Father, Mother, Siblings, or Friends

Beloved, allow Papa God to reveal the lies and tricks of the devil pertaining to your natural relationships and how they have impacted your relationship with Papa God, Jesus Christ, and the Holy Spirit.

The role of the natural father is to provide: Protection – To keep you safe; Provision – To meet all your physical needs; and Identity – To shape and mold your uniqueness, character, and personality,

The role of the natural mother is to provide: Comfort – To console you; Nurturing – To care for and encourage your growth and development; and Teaching – To educate you in all things.

The role of siblings and friends is to provide: Companionship – Friendship.

If you're natural father, mother, siblings, and friends have failed in any of these areas, it will show up in your relationships with Papa God, Jesus Christ, and the Holy Spirit.

Activation Instructions:

1. Ask God to reveal the lies and tricks of the devil in relation to your relationships.

2. Forgive and release others and yourself.

3. Ask God to reveal His truth pertaining to your natural relationships.

4. Close your eyes and visualize entering the throne room of Papa God. Allow Him to show you how He views you, Selah!

5. Make sure to journal your throne room encounters with Papa God.

ACTIVATION 2

The Windows of the Eyes

(7-Day Activation)

For seven days, find a quiet place to meditate on your love for Papa God and His love for you. Close your eyes and focus on looking into your Father's eyes and allowing Him to look into your eyes. In these still moments of gazing at each other, expect an overwhelming outpouring of His love for you. Make sure to journal your Papa God encounters.

FOLLOW-UP

Papa God is yearning for you to pursue Him in intimacy – HE made YOU to crave His LOVE and INTIMACY.

PROPHETIC WORSHIP & SOAKING

"Nothing Else" – Rick Pino (feat. Abbie Gamboa)

"Abba (Spontaneous Worship)" – Jonathan David Helser

"Songs of God's Love (Acoustic Medley)" – Saddleback Worship

"Penuel (Face to Face)" – Rick Pino (Soaking 1.5 Hour)

"Touch of Heaven" – David Funk (Worship Night)

DECREES, DECLARATIONS & PROCLAMATIONS

Share your heart with Papa God by writing Him a LOVE LETTER declaring and proclaiming the depth of your LOVE for HIM.

JOURNALING

I SPOKE TO YOU BEFORE I FORMED YOU

Thank you, Papa God for sharing your heart with me.
I am so grateful for our special time together.

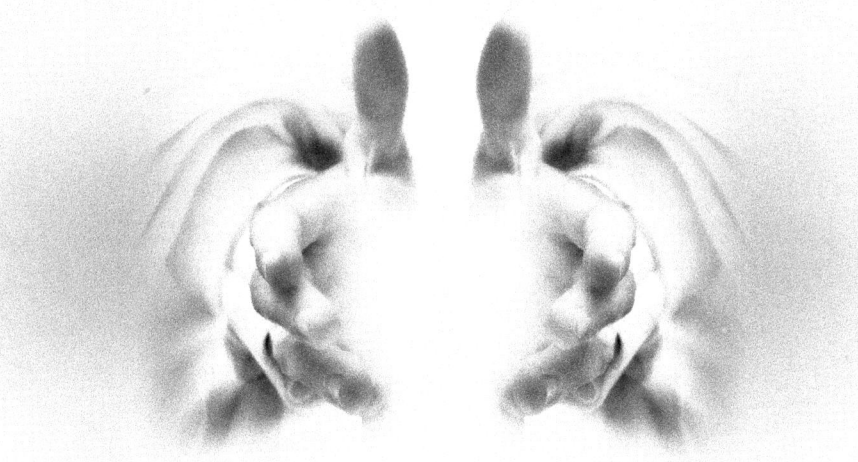

CHAPTER 10

THROUGH THE FRUIT OF THE SPIRIT

QUOTE

"Your manifested fruit is the evidence of your love walk with Papa God." – Melissa Hardy

LOVE NOTE

"My Beloved, I chose to place the very essence of MY CHARACTERISTICS, 'The Fruit of the Spirit,' within you – you are my chosen vessel. I made you to walk in PERFECT LOVE, to live in PERFECT PEACE AND JOY, to extend PATIENCE, GOODNESS, AND KINDNESS, to be FAITHFUL in all things, to operate in GENTLENESS, and to live from a place of obedience, submission, and SELF-CONTROL. Your fruit will reach the lost and restore them back to ME. Your fruit will touch the unlovable. Your fruit will heal the broken-hearted.

Your fruit will be the light to a lost world. Your fruit is ME, and I AM LOVE, PEACE, JOY, PATIENCE, GOODNESS, KINDNESS, FAITHFULNESS, GENTLENESS, AND SELF-CONTROL; therefore, so are you, My Beloved.

I love you, Papa God."

THE MESSAGE

Cultivating the Fruit of the Spirit

"But the fruit of the Spirit [the result of His presence within us] is love [unselfish concern for others], joy, [inner] peace, patience [not the ability to wait, but how we act while waiting], kindness, goodness, faithfulness, gentleness, self-control. Against such things there is no law." (Galatians 5:22-23, AMP)

Beloved, to truly be perfect even as God in Heaven is perfect, you must diligently cultivate and develop the Fruit of the Spirit that resides within you. The Fruit of the Spirit is the very essence of God's characteristics. Beloved, God chose to place His Characteristics – His very Nature – in you, for His will and glory.

"You have not chosen Me, but I have chosen you and I have appointed and placed and purposefully planted you, so that you would go and bear fruit and keep on bearing, and that your fruit will remain and be lasting, so that whatever you ask of the Father in My name [as My representative] He may give to you." (John 15:16, AMP)

Your relationship with Papa God is cultivated when you live by the Fruit of the Spirit. The precious gift of the Fruit of the Spirit is to help you become more like your Papa God. Walking in the

Fruit of the Spirit manifests Papa God's transforming power of love in your life and in those you interact with. Your daily walk should be a demonstration of the Fruit of the Spirit – this is how others see the love of Papa God through you.

It is through the process of cultivation that you surrender your whole self to be refined in the area of the Fruit of the Spirit. When you are weak in the Fruit of the Spirit, it is a direct reflection of your relationship with Papa God. Your lack of relationship will be visible in how you react to life's situations and your relationships with others. In order to fulfill your Kingdom calling in a way that is pleasing to Papa God, you must be willing to allow Papa God to develop and mature the Fruit of the Spirit within you daily.

FRUIT OF THE SPIRIT

Love – God is LOVE! The Word of God is laced with the message of love – for God created you out of love. God sent His Son Jesus to redeem and restore you back to Him out of His love for you. Everything God is and does is based in love. Beloved, He created you in His image – love Him as He loves you – love others and yourself as He loves you – and yes, love your enemies as He loves you.

> *"Love endures with patience and serenity, love is kind and thoughtful, and is not jealous or envious; love does not brag and is not proud or arrogant. It is not rude; it is not self-seeking, it is not provoked [nor overly sensitive and easily angered]; it does not take into account a wrong endured. It does not rejoice at injustice, but rejoices with the truth [when right and truth prevail]. Love bears all things [regardless of what comes], believes all things [looking*

for the best in each one], hopes all things [remaining steadfast during difficult times], endures all things [without weakening]. Love never fails [it never fades nor ends]. But as for prophecies, they will pass away; as for tongues, they will cease; as for the gift of special knowledge, it will pass away." (1 Corinthians 13:4-8, AMP)

Joy – Joy is connected to receiving the love of God. When you accept God's love, you will live from a place of deep inner joy, with a joyful heart – rejoicing and trusting God in all things.

"May the God of hope fill you with all joy and peace in believing [through the experience of your faith] that by the power of the Holy Spirit you will abound in hope and overflow with confidence in His promises." (Romans 15:13, AMP)

Peace – Beloved, the peace of God already resides within you, so there is no need to pray or ask God for peace. You must completely trust God and allow peace to flow in your Soul, your mind (thoughts), heart (emotions), and your will (decisions). Peace will allow you to be content (satisfied), secure (confident and vulnerable), and unmoved… free of trouble… Christ-like. Walking in your Kingdom calling allows you to live from a place of peace because your focus is on His will and not your own.

"Now may the Lord of peace Himself grant you His peace at all times and in every way [that peace and spiritual well-being that comes to those who walk with Him, regardless of life's circumstances]. The Lord be with you all." (2 Thessalonians 3:16, AMP)

Patience (Longsuffering) – You must have the ability to withstand under pressure with a kind, caring, and loving heart, possessing an even-tempered mind, not complaining or being easily provoked to anger. Patience will allow you to have a peaceful demeanor with yourself and others.

> *"Constantly rejoicing in hope [because of our confidence in Christ], steadfast and patient in distress, devoted to prayer [continually seeking wisdom, guidance, and strength]."* (Romans 12:12, AMP)

Kindness and Goodness – The physical appearances of "kindness" and "goodness" are very similar. Together, they characterize how you act toward others. Throughout the Bible, we see powerful actions of God's kindness and goodness toward His children.

> *"Be kind and helpful to one another, tender-hearted [compassionate, understanding], forgiving one another [readily and freely], just as God in Christ also forgave you."* (Ephesians 4:32, AMP)

Faith – Faith is placing your trust in God and exercising your faith – believing in what you cannot see. Think about how much faith God has in you, despite your circumstances. His faith sees you in your true identity – the "I Spoke to You" before I created you and placed you in your Mother's womb.

> *"So then faith cometh by hearing, and hearing by the word of God."* (Romans 10:17, KJV)

> *"So faith comes from hearing [what is told], and what is heard comes by the [preaching of the] message concerning Christ."* (Romans 10:17, AMP)

Gentleness – Your brother Jesus modeled the fruit of gentleness and love as He ministered to people. Gentleness is laced with kindness (compassion, sympathy, and thoughtfulness), friendliness, and consideration (concern, respect, and reflection). Jesus took a compassionate, loving approach towards people's weaknesses and infirmities. He spoke truth in a gentle manner that pierced people's hearts. Your gentleness in handling God's most precious children is a sign of maturity.

> *"Come to Me, all who are weary and heavily burdened [by religious rituals that provide no peace], and I will give you rest [refreshing your souls with salvation]. Take My yoke upon you and learn from Me [following Me as My disciple], for I am gentle and humble in heart, and you will find rest (renewal, blessed quiet) for your souls. For My yoke is easy [to bear] and My burden is light."* (Matthew 11:28-30, AMP)

Self-Control – Self-Control is not just about controlling your behavior (your thoughts and emotions) but also about not resisting God and His Word. Jesus is a shining example of living a life of self-control in order to fulfill the Father's will, dying for your sins so that you would have eternal life.

> *"Like a city that is broken down and without walls [leaving it unprotected] is a man who has no self-control over his spirit [and sets himself up for trouble]."* (Proverbs 25:28, AMP)

HOW TO CULTIVATE THE FRUIT

To cultivate the fruit, you must be willing to spend time with your Father by reading the Word of God and learning about the Life of Jesus. In His presence, you will understand how deeply

He loves you and how that love transforms and sanctifies you. Your fruit will leave a lasting impact on everyone around you. If you're not sure where to start, ask your Father for guidance – He already knows the condition of your heart and the plans for increasing your fruitfulness.

> *My Story: Cultivating the Fruit of the Spirit is an area in my life that I have been working on for years. And because of my love for Papa God and my desire to be more like Him, I chose to cultivate the Fruit of the Spirit daily. For me personally, I have found that partnering with Papa God encourages the following when it comes to cultivating the Fruit of the Spirit:*
>
> *Transparency – I must first be transparent with myself before I can be transparent with Papa God and others.*
>
> *Accountability – The Word of God and the Holy Spirit encourage me to be accountable to Papa God and others when it comes to my words and actions.*
>
> *Healing – Cultivating the Fruit of the Spirit causes me to routinely revisit the operating room, which manifests spiritual and physical growth.*
>
> *I am so thankful Papa God loves me so much that He freely gives me grace and mercy to grow in the area of the Fruit of the Spirit.*

ACTIVATION

Heart Check-Up

A Time of Thanksgiving – Think about the areas of fruitfulness in your life and give thanks to God for these wonderful things.

Heart Check-Up – Then consider and journal areas of your life that lack fruit.

Heart Tune-Up – Allow Papa God to address your areas of weakness and heal areas of your heart.

Activation – Ask Papa God for strategies on how you can increase your fruitfulness.

FOLLOW-UP

When your life lacks manifested fruit, it is evidence of the absence of relationship with Papa God and of broken areas of the heart. For the Fruit of the Spirit flows from the HEART OF GOD through you, His chosen vessel. Continue to allow Papa God (in your encounters with Him) to cultivate your fruit, and practice, practice, practice living from the Fruit of the Spirit. When your life bears fruit, it brings Papa God so much pleasure.

PROPHETIC WORSHIP & SOAKING

"Nothing Else" – Rick Pino (feat. Abbie Gamboa)

"Abba (Spontaneous Worship)" – Jonathan David Helser

"Refiner" – TRIBL Music (feat. Chandler Moore & Steffany Gretzinger)

"New Wine" – Maverick City Music (feat. Montel Moore & DOE)

DECREES, DECLARATIONS & PROCLAMATIONS

I DECREE, "I AM" who God says "I AM," His Beloved creation whom He commands to BE FRUITFUL and to multiply; therefore, I am blessed with a fruitful life.

I DECLARE, Lord, YOU said in YOUR Word that I abide in Christ, and therefore I manifest the Fruit of the Spirit: Love, Joy, Peace, Patience, Kindness, Goodness, Faithfulness, Gentleness, and Self-control.

I PROCLAIM, God created me to be a fruitful vine, always producing and bearing good fruit.

JOURNALING

I Spoke to You Before I Formed You

Thank you, Papa God for sharing your heart with me.
I am so grateful for our special time together.

Section V
The Birthing Room

"It is time to birth the very words Papa God Spoke over you before time." – Melissa Hardy

Come Forth Butterfly

CHAPTER 11

PREPARING FOR BIRTH

QUOTE

"Beloved, you were made to BIRTH
HEAVEN to Earth." – Melissa Hardy

LOVE NOTE

"My Beloved, the birthing process can be quite painful, and you will encounter many trials, attacks, and challenges. Why? Because the devil does not want you to birth your calling, the 'I SPOKE TO YOU' before I formed you and placed you in your Mother's womb. The devil will do anything and everything to stop you from BIRTHING HEAVEN on Earth. My Beloved, you are in the fight of your life – stay focused on ME and know that you have already won.

I love you, Papa God."

THE MESSAGE

Back to the Operating Room

Beloved, before you enter into the Birthing Room, Papa God is calling you back to the Operating Room. Why? Because you cannot BIRTH Heaven into the Earth if you are still carrying things or areas that require healing pertaining to your calling. While you have gone through a 30-day healing process, Papa God is saying:

"Beloved, you and I have done a lot of work healing your heart, mind, and physical body; however, it's time to go deeper. Into the deep areas the devil has hidden from you, the ones you don't even know exist. The devil has sown lies you don't even remember... there are roots of unforgiveness you thought were good... and there are generational areas of bondage you are unaware of. These lies, areas of unforgiveness, and areas of generational bondage were the devil's last resort to stop you from BIRTHING YOUR CALLING. Entering into the BIRTHING ROOM without healing these deep wounds is life-threatening to your baby – and may result in hindering the birthing process, miscarriage, abortion, stillbirth, or a premature birth. Beloved, DO NOT enter the BIRTHING ROOM without returning to the Operating Room.

I love You, Papa God."

Entering into the Birthing Room without returning to the Operating Room may impact your calling in the following ways:

Hindrance of the Spirit Birthing Process – causing you to become stuck (unable to move forward) in the birthing process.

Beloved, you're going to have to do something – push through the pain and contractions, allowing Papa God to deal with whatever has caused you to become stuck.

> In the natural – *My story: While giving birth to my daughter (1986), I entered into labor and my cervix dilated to 5 centimeters, and then all of a sudden, everything just stopped. For 48 hours, my cervix remained at 5 centimeters. I WAS STUCK – NOTHING WAS HAPPENING! The doctors released me from the hospital with instructions to do a lot of walking and climbing stairs. No medication or special medical procedures. I had to physically do something, move my body – forcing it to get unstuck – forcing it to move forward.*
>
> *After 12 hours of a lot of walking and climbing steps, my cervix shifted and I was rushed to the hospital. I had dilated to 6 centimeters – then it stopped! I remained in the hospital with instructions to walk up and down the hallways – so I paced the hallway all night. And then at 6:00 a.m., my cervix kicked into high gear and I began to dilate – 7 – 8 – 9 – and finally 10 – we were MOVING FORWARD – THROUGH THE PAIN – THROUGH THE CONTRACTIONS – THROUGH THE PUSHING – WE WERE MOVING FORWARD – AND THEN IT WAS OVER! Heaven arrived to Earth – baby girl took her first earthly breath and began to cry, letting me know, "I AM HERE!"*

Miscarriage – causing you to lose your spiritual baby (calling) due to lies from the devil, unforgiveness, and areas of bondage.

> In the natural, miscarriage normally happens between weeks 1 and 24 of a mother's pregnancy, as a result of

poorly controlled long-term diseases such as diabetes or high blood pressure, fibroids, or problems with the uterus or cervix. A pregnancy may also be impacted by obesity, smoking, using drugs or alcohol, or even drinking lots of caffeine.

Beloved, if you (women or men) have experienced a miscarriage and you are holding Papa God or others responsible, now is the time to forgive and let go. Allow Papa God to heal this area of your life.

Abortion – causing you to abort your spiritual baby (putting to death, killing, or destroying your calling) due to lies from the devil, unforgiveness, and areas of bondage.

In the natural, a woman decides to terminate her pregnancy, resulting in the death of the baby (embryo or fetus).

Beloved, Papa God has a lot to say about abortions and the preborn in His Word. His Word proclaims the highest importance of protecting life in the womb – read Luke 1 (ERV) and Psalm 51 (ERV).

"You formed the way I think and feel. You put me together in my mother's womb. I praise you because you made me in such a wonderful way. I know how amazing that was! You could see my bones grow as my body took shape, hidden in my mother's womb. You could see my body grow each passing day. You listed all my parts, and not one of them was missing. Your thoughts are beyond my understanding. They cannot be measured! If I could count them, they would be more than all

the grains of sand. But when I finished, I would have just begun." (Psalm 139:13-18, ERV)

In the following scriptures, Jeremiah 1:4-5 and Isaiah 49:1, we see Papa God place great importance on the value of life in the womb and care for preborn children.

"Now the word of the Lord came to me, saying, 'Before I formed you in the womb I knew you, and before you were born I consecrated you; I appointed you a prophet to the nations." (Jeremiah 1:4-5, ESV)

"The Lord called me from the womb, from the body of my mother he named my name." (Isaiah 49:1b, ESV)

Beloved, if you (women or men) have had an experience with an abortion and Papa God has not yet healed your heart, now is the time to ask for forgiveness and allow Him to make you whole in this area of your life.

Stillbirth – causing your spiritual baby to be born dead due to lies from the devil, unforgiveness, and areas of bondage.

> In the natural, a stillbirth is the death of a baby in the womb after week 20 of the mother's pregnancy or during delivery. In some cases, the death is unexplainable; however, in about two-thirds of cases, there are problems with the placenta or umbilical cord, high blood pressure, infections, birth defects, or poor lifestyle choices (drugs, alcohol, smoking, etc.).
>
> Beloved, if you (women or men) have experienced a stillbirth and you are holding Papa God or others

responsible, now is the time to forgive and let go. Allow Papa God to heal this area of your life.

Premature Birth – causing your spiritual baby to be born early due to lies from the devil, unforgiveness, and areas of bondage. Beloved, getting ahead of Papa God when it comes to the spiritual birthing of your calling can cause you to birth prematurely, resulting in you having major challenges in the execution of your calling, or even your calling not surviving.

In the natural, babies born before 24 weeks of pregnancy are called premature. Premature babies can have serious long-term health problems at birth and later in life, and have a 50 percent chance of surviving.

Beloved, this is a very critical (dangerous, serious, life-threatening, and perilous) moment of time in your life. I pray you surrender to Papa God's plea and return to the Operating Room prior to proceeding forward.

ACTIVATION

Operating Room

(7-Day Activation)

Beloved, Papa God is calling you back into the operating room for seven days – feel free to reread Chapter 7 if you'd like. During this time of deep, deep, deep healing and stripping away, more lies will be replaced with Papa God's truth and additional chains of bondage and unforgiveness will be broken. Papa God knows all your secrets and the depth of your battle wounds. Activation instructions:

1. Select a time of day when you will not be interrupted and can spend as much time as needed in the operating room with Papa God.

2. Daily prepare your heart through prayer, worship, and the Word of God, through the leading of the Holy Spirit.

3. Release and surrender yourself to Papa God. The key to healing is being honest and vulnerable with Papa God.

4. Daily ask Papa God these questions and journal His responses and your healing journey.

    ~ Ask Papa God, "What do you want to operate on today?" Sometimes Papa God will stay in one area for a few days; just follow His lead.

    ~ Ask yourself, "Why am I dealing with this?" Being vulnerable and honest with yourself and Papa God can be painful. Be encouraged, freedom awaits you on the other side.

    ~ Ask Papa God, "Why am I dealing with this?" Be open to hear His heart and voice!

    ~ Ask Papa God, "What can I do today and moving forward to improve in this area?" Be open to receive His correction and instructions. He may require you to fast for a certain time period with specific instructions; read a particular scripture or listen to a certain song; or even speak with your pastor.

5. Through your 7-day healing process, Papa God may reveal areas in your life requiring in-depth Christian counseling. Papa God knows your healing process from the beginning to the end; He is the Alpha "the beginning" and the Omega "the end." Beloved, surrender and trust Papa God and His process of healing for you.

6. Beloved, Papa God may require you to remain in the Operating Room longer than seven days; follow the leading of the Holy Spirit.

7. Kindly, do not continue to read "I SPOKE TO YOU" until you complete your seven-day healing activation or Papa God releases you to do so.

FOLLOW-UP

Preparing for the BIRTHING ROOM can be just as painful – if not more so – than actually giving BIRTH. Beloved, I am so proud of all you have accomplished up to this point of "I SPOKE TO YOU." I can feel your baby leaping in my own womb – can you feel your baby leaping in your womb? I can feel your baby beginning to push with great force and strength – can you feel your baby beginning to push? Beloved, the time has come for you to enter into the Birthing Room. The time has come for you to birth what Papa God "SPOKE TO YOU" before He formed you and placed you in your Mother's womb.

PROPHETIC WORSHIP & SOAKING

"Nothing Else" – Rick Pino (feat. Abbie Gamboa)

"Abba (Spontaneous Worship)" – Jonathan David Helser

The Altar Sessions (Live Volume 1) – Rick Pino

"You Restore Everything" – Rick Pino (feat. Abbie Gamboa)

"Learning to Be Loved by You" – Melissa Helser

"I Am Your Beloved" & "Running Home" – Jonathan & Melissa Helser

"New Wine" – Maverick City Music (feat. Montel Moore & DOE)

"I Speak Jesus" – Charity Gayle (feat. Steven Musso)

"When I Lock Eyes with You" – Maverick City and UPPERROOM

"He Knows My Name" – Francesca Battistelli (Official Music Video)

DECREES, DECLARATIONS & PROCLAMATIONS

In preparation to enter into the Birthing Room, spend some time reading these scriptures in different versions and Selah! Then write your own personalized decrees, declarations, and proclamations and post them where you can see and read them daily.

"Before I formed you (BELOVED) *in the womb I knew you, and before you were born I consecrated you; I appointed you a prophet (YOUR CALLING) to the nations."* (Jeremiah 1:5, ESV, alterations mine)

"And after you (BELOVED) *have suffered a little while, the God of all grace, who has CALLED YOU to his eternal glory in Christ, will himself* (PAPA GOD) *restore, confirm, strengthen, and establish you* (BELOVED).*"* (1 Peter 5:10, ESV, alterations mine)

"A woman (YOU, BELOVED), *when she is in labor, has pain because her time [to give birth] has come; but when she has given birth to the child* (CALLING), *she no longer remembers the anguish because of her joy that a child (CALLING) has come into the world."* (John 16:21, AMP, alterations mine)

JOURNALING

Thank you, Papa God for sharing your heart with me.
I am so grateful for our special time together.

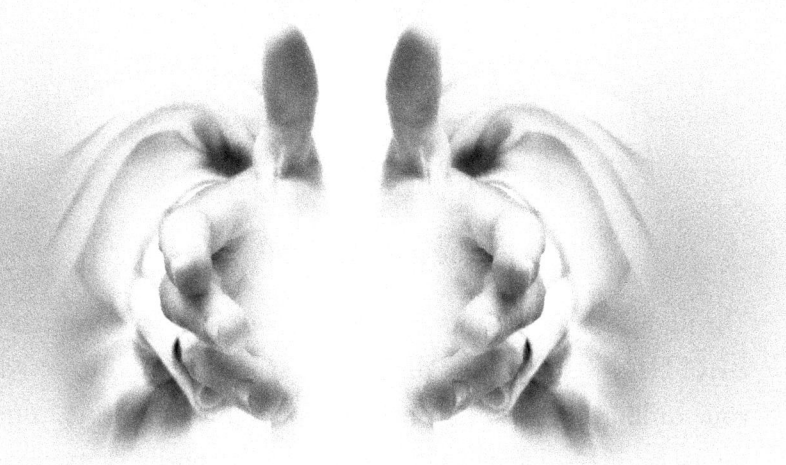

CHAPTER 12

It's Time

QUOTE

"Beloved, in the heavenly realm, you have already BIRTHED HEAVEN to Earth – you are only reliving Kingdom history." – Melissa Hardy

LOVE NOTE

"My Beloved, The time has come for you to BIRTH what 'I SPOKE TO YOU' Before I formed you and placed you in your Mother's womb. The time has come for you to PUSH...

PUSH, PUSH, PUSH, My Beloved

BIRTH HEAVEN TO EARTH.

I love you, Papa God."

THE MESSAGE

The Birthing Room

Throughout your time on earth, you may experience the BIRTHING ROOM at different seasons of your life based on your calling. Depending on what you're birthing, your time in the BIRTHING ROOM could be days, months, or even years. Papa God may require you to birth your full calling in segments (parts, sections). Every birthing experience is different and unique based on the calling. Keys to the BIRTHING ROOM:

Move only under the leading of Papa God's timing and not yours.

Never, never, never follow someone else's birthing process.

Keep your eyes on Papa God (looking up) and not on the trials and challenges (looking down).

Stay rooted and grounded in the Word of God.

Live from the PRESENCE OF GOD – Prayed Up and Worship Down.

Decree, Declare, and Proclaim Papa God's promises to you.

Don't take – I repeat, don't take unauthorized people into the Birthing Room – seek Papa God when it comes to sharing your calling and the birthing process.

Live from the Throne Room – it is already finished – you are only reliving Kingdom history.

Walk in your Papa God-given Power and Authority!

Beloved, remember, the birthing process can be quite painful and you will encounter many trials, attacks, and challenges. Why? Because the devil does not want you to birth your calling, the "I SPOKE TO YOU" before Papa God formed you and placed you in your Mother's womb. The devil will do anything and everything to stop you from BIRTHING HEAVEN on Earth. Beloved, you are in the fight of your life – stay focused on Papa God and know that you have already BIRTHED HEAVEN to Earth – you are only reliving Kingdom history.

Beloved, I want to share my birthing testimony with you, not to scare you or to discourage you from entering into the Birthing Room, but to encourage you and remind you that Papa God has prepared you to enter into the Birthing Room. You and Papa God spent countless hours in the Operating Room – healing layer by layer, removing the lies of the devil, healing issues of unforgiveness, and destroying areas of bondage. The healing process is critical for you to birth and fulfill your calling. While I was writing "I SPOKE TO YOU," there were several times when Papa God required me to return to the operating room to deal with areas of brokenness that were hindering my birthing process. I found myself stuck – unable to move forward! Through my willingness to return to the Operating Room, I was able to birth "I SPOKE TO YOU."

> *My Story – From the moment I said yes to Papa God to birth His book "I SPOKE TO YOU: Before I Formed You," the trials, attacks, and challenges began. Over the last eight months, my husband Rodney and I have been under extreme spiritual warfare. While Papa God has chosen me to author His book, both Rodney and I have been under attack because we live our lives as one in*

covenant with Papa God. Because of our oneness and our "yes" to fulfill the calling on our lives, the devil has attacked us from so many different directions.

- Throughout these eight months, the devil attacked me physically and mentally:

  - Allergic Bronchial Asthma and Sinus infection, which went on for months – bronchial inflammation, which resulted in severe coughing, headaches, shortness of breath, wheezing, and chest pain.

  - Carpal Tunnel, Golfer's and Tennis Elbow, and Shoulder Pain – several flare-ups, so severe at times that I could not move my arms to write or type.

  - Breast Issue – during my annual checkup, the doctor found a lump in my breast, which resulted in numerous tests; thankfully, it was diagnosed as a cyst.

  - Throughout the whole writing process, the devil attacked me mentally through family members and employees within my work organization.

  - The devil would create situations trying to bring divisions and confusion between my husband and me.

  - The devil would constantly question my identity (Papa God's author) and the calling on my life. Yes, beloved, the devil will talk to you – remember, his goal is to cause you to abort your calling. You have to hold on to the very words Papa God "SPOKE TO YOU" and not be moved. This will require you to use your power and authority, and command the devil to shut his mouth.

- *Throughout the eight months, I hindered my own birthing process:*
  - *I battled the spirit of failure – dealing with writer's block and feeling unworthy to write Papa God's book.*
  - *I battled with the spirit of quitting – feeling like a failure as I watched the other authors in my cohort continue to progress forward in the birthing process. Beloved, the fourth week of May 2022, our final draft manuscripts were due, but I had only written 50 percent of the book. Papa God called me back into the operating room, and it was during this time of intimacy that He revealed I did not completely trust Him. My inability to trust Him completely had been hindering the birthing process. In that very moment, I laid down my life and surrendered, and a peace of God came bubbling out. And within six weeks, Papa God and I flowed freely in partnership – and the book was completed.*
- *During this time, I battled and overcome a great amount of other personal challenges.*
  - *In November and December 2021, an immediate family member was battling with suicidal tendencies, multiple personalities, and witchcraft due to years of physical, emotional, and verbal abuse. Our family spent weeks dealing with mental health facilities and our family member, who refused mental health care.*
  - *In January 2022, our whole household tested positive for COVID – we battled for weeks to get well.*

- *In February and April 2022, I experienced writer's block — yes, writer's block is real and very frustrating.*

- *In March 2022, a co-worker departed the organization abruptly, which resulted in me covering four areas of responsibility for three months; the magnitude of the workload mentally and physically drained me.*

- *From March to May 2022, I was subjected to external co-workers creating a hostile work environment for myself and our internal team.*

- *In April 2022, another immediate family member was battling with suicidal tendencies due to severe PTSD, refusing mental health care.*

- *In April 2022, Rodney, who has been battling liver cancer for 18 months, received a doctor report stating they found two new cancerous tumors.*

- *In May 2022, Rodney underwent his fifth liver surgery.*

- *In May 2022, our air conditioner unit decided its life expectancy was up — we had to purchase a whole new AC unit.*

- *In May 2022, we received a notice from our propane company stating, "Sorry, we didn't calculate your bill correctly for the last 12 months, and you owe us $1,200.00 — immediately."*

- *In May 2022, another immediate family member attempted suicide due to COVID pandemic isolation,*

> *depression, and anxiety. We are so thankful our family member was and is protected by the Blood of Jesus Christ and is still with us – and seeking mental health care.*

Papa God would never have placed a calling within you and me if we were not able to withstand, bear, tolerate, and endure the Birthing Room process. Beloved, I can see your baby taking their first earthly breath – can you see your baby breathing? I can hear your baby crying, announcing their arrival – can you hear your baby crying? I can see your baby crawling, then walking, and finally running in full maturity – can you see your baby fulling their purpose? Beloved, Papa God has His hand stretched out to you, and He is calling you into the Birthing Room.

ACTIVATION

The Birthing Room

"My Beloved, Oh, how I have waited for this moment in time. Come and take My hand, let us enter into the Birthing Room together.

I love you, Papa God."

Activation instructions:

1. Select a time of day when you will not be interrupted and can spend as much time as needed in the birthing room with Papa God.

2. Prepare your heart through prayer, worship, and the Word of God, through the leading of the Holy Spirit.

3. Release and surrender yourself to Papa God.

4. Make sure to journal your birthing process.

5. I highly encourage you to continue reading "I SPOKE TO YOU" while you're in the Birthing Room. The Legacy chapters will help you connect the birthing of your calling to the creating and passing of your legacy (calling) on to the next generation.

FOLLOW-UP

Beloved, enter into the Birthing Room with great expectation and remember the following keys to birthing:

~ Keep the very words Papa God "SPOKE TO YOU" before He formed you and placed you in your Mother's womb in your heart and before your eye gates.

~ Stay connected to Papa God through prayer, fasting, worship, and His Word.

~ Move only under the leading of Papa God's timing and not yours – His process and not yours – His will and not yours.

~ Return to the operating room under the leading of the Holy Spirit.

~ Surrender and fully trust Papa God with the calling He has placed within you.

~ Live from the Throne Room – it is already finished – you are only reliving Kingdom history.

PROPHETIC WORSHIP & SOAKING

"Nothing Else" – Rick Pino (feat. Abbie Gamboa)

"Abba (Spontaneous Worship)" – Jonathan David Helser

"Earth to God" – John Rich

"Rattle!" –Elevation Worship (Official Lyric Video)

"Graves Into Gardens" – Elevation Worship (feat. Brandon Lake), Live

DECREES, DECLARATIONS & PROCLAMATIONS

Daily, continue to read the decrees, declarations and proclamations you created in Chapter 11. Throughout the Birthing Room process, Papa God will illuminate additional scriptures for you to add to your list of decrees, declarations, and proclamations.

JOURNALING

I SPOKE TO YOU Before I Formed You

Thank you, Papa God for sharing your heart with me.
I am so grateful for our special time together.

Section VI
Generations To Come

"Everything created on the Earth is MY legacy, for I am the King of Kings – creator of the World." – Melissa Hardy

Kingdom Building

CHAPTER 13

BUILDING LEGACY

QUOTE

"I am the master builder – you are My vessel of Legacy." – Melissa Hardy

LOVE NOTE

"My Beloved, Your legacy on earth is only a manifestation of Kingdom history: You are only reliving what has already taken place in Heaven. You are a conduit (a channel, canal, pipeline, and outlet) from Heaven to Earth – Plug & Play – Plug yourself into Heaven and Re-Play what has already been done in Heaven on Earth – Plug & Play! Your responsibility is to Plug & Play what 'I SPOKE TO YOU' before I formed you and placed you in your Mother's womb. Your responsibility is to partner with Me, to fulfill the calling I have placed inside you, Beloved. The very purpose of your creation is to dominate the Earth and to bring Me Glory. Plug & Play, You were made for this!

I love you, Papa God."

THE MESSAGE

Beloved, in the beginning, you were created in the very image of God.

> *"Then God said, 'Let Us (Father, Son, Holy Spirit) make man in Our image, according to Our likeness [not physical, but a spiritual personality and moral likeness]; and let them have complete authority over the fish of the sea, the birds of the air, the cattle, and over the entire earth, and over everything that creeps and crawls on the earth.' So God created man in His own image, in the image and likeness of God He created him; male and female He created them."* (Genesis 1:26-27, AMP)

God created you to build Kingdom Legacy and to dominate (rule over and control) the Earth!

> *"And God blessed them [granting them certain authority] and said to them, 'Be fruitful, multiply, and fill the earth, and subjugate it [putting it under your power]; and rule over (dominate) the fish of the sea, the birds of the air, and every living thing that moves upon the earth.'"* (Genesis 1:28, AMP)

The purpose of your Kingdom Legacy is to dominate your sphere of influence through your God-given calling (purpose, destiny, and assignment). If God created you to dominate the Earth, then He has equipped you with everything you need to fulfill your calling. Beloved, you have the potential, capacity, and ability to dominate because God placed it within you.

You may still be questioning your own natural ability to walk out your calling. Beloved, God is not requiring you to fulfill His mandate on your life out of your own ability. God is looking for you to partner with Him as you walk out "I SPOKE TO YOU before I formed you and placed you in your Mother's womb." Beloved, remember God's words: *"Your legacy – walking out your calling on earth – is only a manifestation of Kingdom history: You are only reliving what has already taken place in Heaven."*

> *"That which is has already been, and that which will be has already been, for God seeks what has passed by [so that history repeats itself]." (Ecclesiastes 3:15, AMP)*

> *"That which is, already has been. And that which will be, has already been. For God allows the same things to happen again." (Ecclesiastes 3:15, NIV)*

God is the beginning (THE ALPHA - THE CREATOR) and the end (THE OMEGA – THE FINISHER), therefore everything on earth has already been created, executed, and completed in Heaven. God requires you to partner with Him, you are a conduit (a channel, canal, pipeline, and an outlet) from Heaven to Earth –

Plug & Play! God is looking for you to Plug yourself into Heaven and Re-Play what has already been done in Heaven on Earth – Plug & Play!

> *My Story: I fully understand what you are going through or experiencing as you grapple with fulfilling your calling. The magnitude of the calling, when placed on your shoulders, can become overwhelming. Several times as I wrote "I SPOKE TO YOU," I shifted the responsibility of completing the book from Papa God to myself. I placed the responsibility on my shoulders! I would find*

myself making comments like *"How am **I** going to finish this book?"* or *"**I am** so behind, **I'll** never catch up."* The weight of writing the book out of **My Own Ability** became too much for me to bear. I would find myself experiencing writer's block for weeks, which led to frustration – which led to stress – which led to a low immune system – which led to sickness (COVID, allergies, uncontrolled coughs and wheezing, headaches, insomnia, and intestinal issues). During these times of weakness and brokenness, Papa God would show up in the middle of the night and minister to my heart.

Through His love and correction, He would redirect my focus back to Him and my writing would flow freely – until my next moment of weakness (shifting back to self). I keep asking myself, "Why do I keep getting on this same roller coaster ride?" In my mind, I knew I needed to stay focused on Papa God, but in my heart, I kept reverting back to trusting in my own ability (self). I did not realize I still had a trust issue – I had not fully surrendered my life and calling to Papa God.

In my brokenness, I attended the Voice of the Prophets gathering and saturated myself in His presence. And as I laid it at the altar, Papa God healed this area of brokenness. One of the things Papa God said to me was, "When something is impossible, daughter, it doesn't belong to you – it belongs to Me." It was in that very moment that I received this life-changing revelation – everything that Papa God has placed in me and called me to do doesn't belong to me – it belongs to HIM! In that moment of surrendering to Papa God, I chose to trust Him with my whole heart. I reached for His hand in partnership, and together we completed 50 percent of *"I SPOKE TO YOU"* in six weeks.

Beloved, your legacy process has been uniquely designed just for you. You are the only one who can do what God "SPOKE TO YOU." It's important not to compare yourself to others or to follow their legacy process. For example, if Papa God is asking you to author His book, your process, challenges, and writing style would not be the same as mine. Following Papa God's legacy process will lead you to victory.

BIBLICAL EXAMPLES

Beloved, your Plug and Play – your Legacy Master Plan has been exclusively designed by Papa God based on your unique calling. Simply surrender to Papa God – partner with Him and walk out your calling. Let's look at a few biblical examples and see how they walked out their calling.

Noah (Genesis 6:5-22, AMP) – Noah had to do what God instructed him to do, even though it didn't make sense and others ridiculed him. God gave Noah very in-depth instructions about his calling: exactly how to build the ark and how to fill the ark. Noah and his family followed God's directions and survived the flood. They witnessed God's eternal promise (through a rainbow) to never destroy the earth by flood.

> Beloved, you will not obey God perfectly in your life and calling. But the more you obey out of your love for Him, the more fully you will experience His joy and fruitfulness.

Abraham (Genesis 12:1-5, AMP) – Abraham received God's instructions to leave his home and extended family; however, he had no idea where he was going or the difficulties he would face to become a blessing to all the families of the earth. God told Abraham WHAT to do (leave) before showing him the WHERE (to go).

> Beloved, you know God is calling you to do something, but you may doubt (hesitate, walk in uncertainty) because you don't know how you will accomplish the assignment. Do not fear – this is normal – just step out (do something) in faith and trust God.

Rahab (Joshua 2:1-24, AMP) – Rahab was a prostitute and a citizen of a country at war with the Israelites. She knew nothing about the Israelites' God and merely protected the Israelite spies in order to save herself. But God! In the process, she learned about God and declared her faith by recognizing God as the supreme God in the heavens and earth. God used Rahab to fulfill His promise to the Israelites and to preserve the family lineage of Jesus.

> Beloved, God will give you victory in your life and calling, regardless of your past, to accomplish His will (purpose) for His glory.

ACTIVATION

Developing Legacy!

(14-Day Activation)

Papa God wants you to glean from your brothers and sisters who have gone before you in walking out their calling. Reading their stories and answering the associated questions will help you navigate through developing your own legacy.

Activation Instructions:

Day 1 – Read Genesis 6:5-22, AMP (Noah's calling)

Question: What is God asking you to do that doesn't make any sense to you?

Your Response: _____

_____

_____

Day 2 – Read Genesis 12:1-5, AMP (Abraham's calling)

Question: Has God asked you to do something without giving you the HOW TO instructions? If so, what does He want you to do while you wait on His instructions?

Your Response: _____

_____

_____

Day 3 – Read Genesis 37:1-11; 42:6-9; 50:14-21, AMP (Joseph's calling)

Question: How have your mistakes and sins delayed your calling? How do you think God will use your mistakes or sins for His purposes?

Your Response: _____

_____

_____

Day 4 – Read Joshua 1:1-18, AMP (Joshua's calling)

Question: How do you believe God wants to encourage you to be "strong and courageous" when it comes to your calling?

Your Response: _____

_____

_____

Day 5 – Read Joshua 2:1-24, AMP (Rahab's calling)

Question: How do you believe God will give you the victory in your calling in spite of your past? It's important for you to encourage others in the same way.

Your Response: _____

_____

_____

Day 6 – Judges 13:1-7, 24-25; 14:5-6, 18-20; 15:14-15; 16:20-22, AMP (Samson's Calling)

Question: Ask God to show you and help you overcome any habitual sins that will impact the fruitfulness of your calling.

Your Response: _____

_____

_____

Day 7 – 1 Samuel 16:1-13, 17; 17:41-50; Acts 13:22, AMP (David's Calling)

Question: How do you think God wants to encourage you in your calling, especially areas that are still unclear?

Your Response: _____

_____

_____

Day 8 – Read Esther 4:1-17, 9:1, AMP (Esther's Calling)

Question: Have you lost hope in any part of your calling? Seek God for encouragement and the strength to persevere.

Your Response: _____

_____

_____

Day 9 – Read Isaiah 6:8-13, AMP (Isaiah's Calling)

Question: Has God called you to do something that you don't want to do? Have a conversation with God about how you feel and why. Be open to hear God's response and willing to reconsider His request of you.

Your Response: _____

_____

_____

Day 10 – Read Jeremiah 1:3-16, 29:11; Genesis 17:15-17, AMP (Jeremiah's and Abraham's Callings)

Question: Are you struggling with feeling too young or too old for your calling? Again, have a conversation with God, and let His truth become your truth.

Your Response: _____

_____

_____

Day 11 – Read Ezekiel 3:1-14, AMP (Ezekiel's Calling)

Question: Has God communicated your calling (all or part) in an unusual way? Ask Him for clarification.

Your Response: _____

_____

_____

Day 12 – Read Jonah 1:1-3, 13-17; 2:1, 5-10; 3:1-6, AMP (Jonah's Calling)

Question: Beloved, are you running from your calling? Time to talk with God again – ask Him to change your heart and to help you to move forward in fulfilling your calling.

Your Response: _____

_____

_____

Day 13 – Read Luke 1:80; 1 Samuel 2:26; Luke 2:52, AMP (John the Baptist's Calling)

Question: How is God encouraging you to grow physically, emotionally, socially, mentally, and spiritually?

Your Response: _____

_____

_____

Day 14 – Read Acts 9:10-19, AMP (Paul's Calling)

Question: Praise God for your mentors, those who have helped you walk out your calling. Ask God how you can help someone else do the same.

Your Response: _____

_____

_____

FOLLOW-UP

"My Beloved, Your legacy on earth is only a manifestation of Kingdom history: You are only reliving what has already taken place in Heaven. You are a conduit (a channel, canal, pipeline, and outlet) from Heaven to Earth – Plug & Play – Plug yourself into Heaven and Re-Play what has already been done in Heaven on Earth – Plug & Play! Your responsibility is to Plug & Play what 'I SPOKE TO YOU' before I formed you and placed you in your Mother's womb. Your responsibility is to partner with Me to fulfill the calling I have placed inside you, Beloved.

I Love you, Papa God."

PROPHETIC WORSHIP & SOAKING

"Nothing Else" – Rick Pino (feat. Abbie Gamboa)

"Abba (Spontaneous Worship)" – Jonathan David Helser

"Arise (Spontaneous Worship Flow)"
Alberto & Kimberly Rivera

"Caught Up" & "His Holy Name (Spontaneous Worship)" – Soaking Tunes with Alberto

"Worthy of It All" – Burning Ones (feat. Anne Dow & Eric Gilmour)

"Let It Rain" – Eddie James

"Famous For (I Believe)" & "Do It Again (Live)" – Tauren Wells (feat. Jenn Johnson and Christine D'Clario)

DECREES, DECLARATIONS & PROCLAMATIONS

I DECREE, I AM God's CALLED and CHOSEN one, and I live a life that is pleasing to Him and a beacon of light to others, drawing them back to God.

I DECLARE, Lord, YOU said in YOUR Word that I was CALLED and CHOSEN for such a time as this. My life is a reflection of my relationship with You, and my calling is directly connected to leading others back to You.

I PROCLAIM, God CALLED and CHOSE me for such a time as this, and I have already fulfilled my calling and have been welcomed into the Kingdom of my Lord and Savior Jesus Christ – the Kingdom that never ends.

JOURNALING

I Spoke to You Before I Formed You

Thank you, Papa God for sharing your heart with me.
I am so grateful for our special time together.

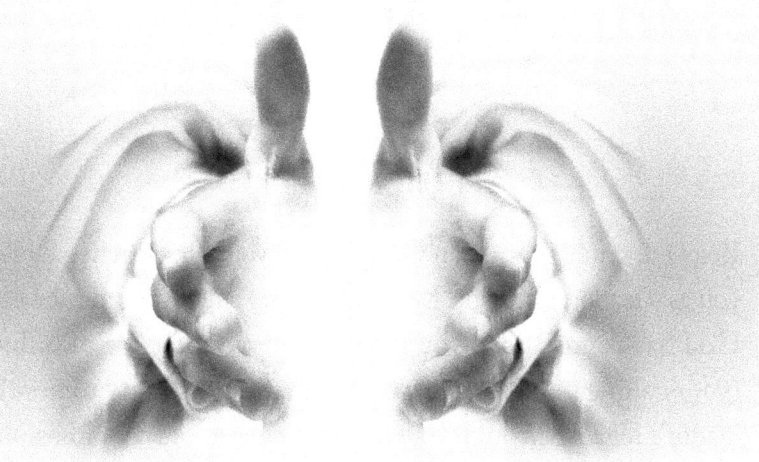

CHAPTER 14

PASSING THROUGH GENERATIONS

QUOTE

"Passing the mantle is the completion of your leg of the race." – Melissa Hardy

LOVE NOTE

"My Beloved, your CALLING is a piece of MY Master Plan – your piece connects to the other pieces. These pieces belong to those who I will divinely connect you with – you are part of a relay team:

Those who have gone before you will serve as your mentor, and you will become their successor…

Those who will come after you, you will mentor, and they will become your successor…

I Love You, Papa God."

THE MESSAGE

Beloved, remember when God created you, He clearly established you as a leader: He said, "Let (your name) rule over… all the earth." God has commanded you to rule from your sphere of influence (your calling). As a leader, you have a responsibility to develop a leader's legacy through one or more successors. God has placed within you the capacity to mentor and influence others through inspiration, created by a passion, inspired by a vision, birthed from a faith, and duplicated by a purpose. Beloved, your calling does not start and stop with you; it is designed to be passed on to the next runner in the relay race – your successor(s).

Prior to the passing of the baton (The Mantle – Your Calling), your successor(s) must be developed through mentor relationships. Every mentor relationship is uniquely different – you will need to seek Papa God for guidance when it comes to selecting your successor(s) and the mentorship requirements and process. Something to keep in mind: based on the magnitude of your calling, God may assign several successors, and the mentorship process for each must be individually tailored. Throughout the Bible, we see leaders mentoring and developing their successors: Abraham mentored Isaac, Jacob mentored Joseph, Moses mentored Joshua, Elijah mentored Elisha, David mentored Solomon, and Jesus mentored the twelve disciples.

MENTORSHIP

"Mentoring" is God's idea. While the word "mentor" never appears in scripture, we see the principle of mentorship active through Biblical relationships. Developing people is extremely important to God, so much so that He sent His own Son, Jesus Christ, to build His legacy through you and your successor(s). The principle of mentorship is multifaceted (multi-layered, complex, and multidimensional):

One-On-One Basis – Naomi mentored Ruth, which led her to marry Boaz. Their marriage union lead to the ancestry of Israel's King David and the Messiah, Jesus Christ.

One Mentor and Multiple Mentees – Papa God mentored Adam and Eve until their fall in the Garden of Eden.

Multiple Mentor Relationships:

Elijah mentored Elisha. Elisha received Elijah's mantle (calling), and he served as Israel's chief prophet (over the Company of Prophets) under God's ultimate power and authority. Elisha performed 11 miracles, which repeatedly showed the power of the true and living God over the supposed kingdom of Baal.

Mordecai mentored Esther. Esther mentored King Artaxerxes, which led to the liberation of God's people, the Israelites.

Jethro mentored Moses. Moses mentored Joshua and the Elders of Israel. Joshua mentored the other remaining leaders of his army. Moses died and transitioned to Heaven. Joshua led the Israelites into the Promised Land of Canaan, fulfilling the promise of God to Abraham.

Eli mentored Samuel. Samuel mentored Saul and David. David became Israel's greatest king. David mentored his army commanders and government officials to establish the Nation of Israel. David also mentored Solomon. Solomon mentored the

Queen of Sheba, who returned to her people with wisdom in the form of Proverbs that applied God's law.

Group Mentorship – Jesus mentored and commissioned (mantled) the twelve disciples (apostles). The apostles mentored hundreds of leaders, including Paul. Paul mentored Titus, Timothy, and many others. Timothy mentored other "faithful men." Ultimately, this mentoring chain was the beginning of establishing our churches of today.

At the appointed time, you will receive instructions from Papa God pertaining to the completion of your calling and the passing of the mantle.

THE CALLING AND MANTLING OF THE DISCIPLES

God placed the responsibility on Jesus Christ to select, develop, and mentor the twelve disciples, for they were CALLED for the Great Commission and the establishment of God's Church on Earth. When Jesus had completed His assignment (His Part of the Race), He prepared the disciples for the passing of the mantle (The Passing of the Baton).

The Disciples Received Instruction from Jesus

> "Listen carefully: I am sending the Promise of My Father [the Holy Spirit] upon you; but you are to remain in the city [of Jerusalem] until you are clothed (fully equipped) with power from on high." (Luke 24:49, AMP)

Jesus Christ Commissioned (Mantled) and Blessed the Disciples

> *"Then He led them out as far as Bethany, and lifted up His hands and blessed them."* (Luke 24:50, AMP)

Jesus Christ Ascended to Heaven

> *"While He was blessing them, He left them and was taken up into heaven."* (Luke 24:51, AMP)

The Disciples Returned to Jerusalem and Waited on God

> *"And they worshiped Him and returned to Jerusalem with great joy [fully understanding that He lives and that He is the Son of God]; and they were continually in the temple blessing and praising God."* (Luke 24:52-53, AMP)

The Filling of the Holy Spirit

> *"When the day of Pentecost had come, they* (THE DISCIPLES) *were all together in one place, and suddenly a sound came from heaven like a rushing violent wind, and it filled the whole house where they were sitting. There appeared to them tongues resembling fire, which were being distributed [among them], and they rested on each one of them [as each person received the Holy Spirit]. And they were all filled [that is, diffused throughout their being] with the Holy Spirit and began to speak in other tongues (different languages), as the Spirit was giving them the ability to speak out [clearly and appropriately]."* (Acts 2:1-4, AMP)

The Disciples' Calling

The disciples were CALLED to go and make Disciples of all the Nations. They were commissioned to create followers of God and to establish His Church. These were the very works Papa God

"SPOKE TO EACH ONE" before He formed them and placed them in their Mothers' wombs.

"Jesus came up and said to them (the disciples), *"All authority (all power of absolute rule) in heaven and on earth has been given to Me. Go therefore and make disciples of all the nations [help the people to learn of Me, believe in Me, and obey My words], baptizing them in the name of the Father and of the Son and of the Holy Spirit, teaching them to observe everything that I have commanded you; and lo, I am with you always [remaining with you perpetually – regardless of circumstance, and on every occasion], even to the end of the age."* (Matthew 28:18-20, AMP)

My Story: My mentorship process to date has been multifaceted. Under the guidance of Papa God, my mentorship journey began while attending Kingdom Bible Institute and Victory Bible College. During these years, Papa God Himself mentored me – it was a time of stripping away the lies of the enemy, healing my heart, building my character, and developing my calling. As I completed this phase of mentorship, Papa God connected me to the Evangelist Keshia Freeland (affectionately known as My Keshia). Over time, we developed a relationship, and He instructed me to enter into her Chosen Treasures Mentorship Program.

Evangelist Keshia Freeland served as one of my midwives, birthing me into my God-ordained destiny. As a member of the Chosen Treasures Mentorship community, I continue to cultivate my calling – as His Chosen Treasures! Most recently, Papa God divinely connected my husband Rodney and me to Pastors Kenneth and Cynthia Barbour for mentorship. I truly believe wholeheartedly that Papa God loves mentorship relationships – because He is a God of covenant relationships.

ACTIVATION 1

Divine Partnerships

1. Spend time praying, fasting, and seeking Papa God for revelation pertaining to your divine partnerships. Beloved, it is very important to understand that this is an ongoing process that may take months or even years. The key is to follow Papa God's instructions at the appointed seasons (time periods).

2. Your Mentor & Mentorship Plan

3. Your Successor(s) & Their Mentorship Plan

4. Under the leading of the Holy Spirit, set a time to meet with your potential mentor and share your heart with them.

5. If they are in agreement with Papa God to mentor you – under the leading of the Holy Spirit, work together to develop your Mentorship Plan.

6. Under the leading of the Holy Spirit, set a time to meet with your potential successor and share your heart with them.

7. If they are in agreement with Papa God for you to serve as their mentor – under the leading of the Holy Spirit, work together to develop their Mentorship Plan.

ACTIVATION 2

Strategic Succession Plan

1. Spend time praying, fasting, and seeking Papa God for revelation pertaining to your Strategic Succession Plan. Beloved, it is very important to follow Papa God's instructions at the appointed seasons (time periods).

2. Develop your Strategic Succession Plan.

3. Your Successor's Mentorship Plan will be included in your Strategic Succession Plan.

FOLLOW-UP

Mentorship

One of the greatest acts of Jesus Christ's leadership was His ability to mentor the disciples.

Jesus Christ understood that His assignment had a shelf life.

Jesus Christ became great by producing leaders who were greater than Himself.

Jesus Christ legacy was to preserve what He had built through mentoring the disciples.

The Passing of the Mantle (Baton)

Jesus Christ's greatest obligation as a leader was the Passing of the Mantle (Baton) to the disciples.

Jesus Christ knew the most important part of His Assignment (Relay) was passing on The Mantle (The Baton) – not just running His part of the race.

Kingdom Legacy

Jesus Christ's greatest gifts to the world were His mentees.

Jesus Christ's leadership success was measured by the success of His successors.

His mentorship ensured that God's legacy did not die when He ascended to Heaven.

Mentoring the disciples freed Jesus Christ to expand His work in Heaven, seated at the right hand of the Father.

PROPHETIC WORSHIP & SOAKING

"Nothing Else" – Rick Pino (feat. Abbie Gamboa)

"Abba (Spontaneous Worship)" – Jonathan David Helser

"Talking to Jesus" – Elevation Worship & Maverick City

"Getting Ready" – Maverick City & UPPERROOM

"We Want More" – Burning Ones (feat. John Wilds & Daniel Kolenda)

DECREES, DECLARATIONS & PROCLAMATIONS

I DECREE, I AM God's CHOSEN LEADER. I have been equipped to mentor and develop my successor, and generations to come will know of our mighty work for the Kingdom of God.

I DECLARE, Lord, YOU said in YOUR Word that generation after generation will stand in awe and tell stories of the mighty works WE (my Successors and I) have accomplished in Your Name and for Your glory.

I PROCLAIM, I have finished my race – my calling – and I have successfully passed the baton on to my successor.

JOURNALING

Thank you, Papa God for sharing your heart with me.
I am so grateful for our special time together.

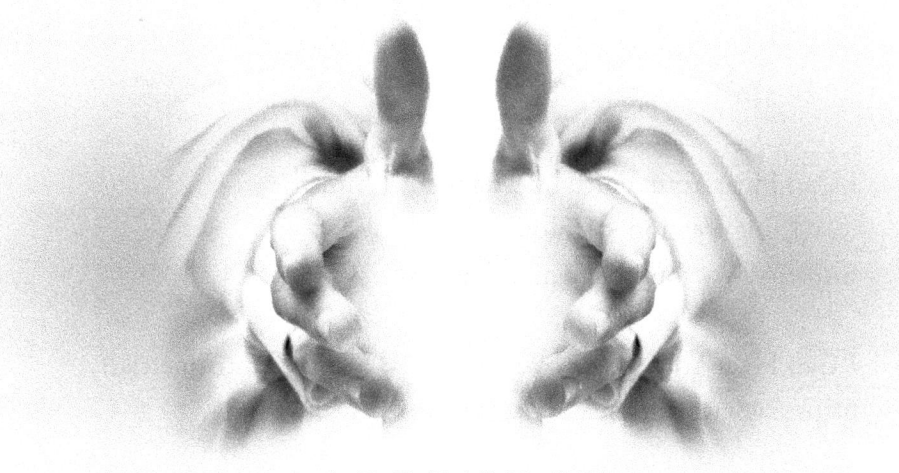

APPENDIX

Prophetic Worship and Soaking Playlist

CHAPTER 1 – HEARING HIS VOICE

Amazing Grace - Video by Gary Downey
    & Song by Judy Collins
https://www.youtube.com/watch?v=CDdvReNKKuk

Nothing Else – Rick Pino (feat. Abbie Gamboa) (Live)
https://www.youtube.com/
    watch?v=if0gY1UNKNo&ab_channel=RickPino

Abba (Spontaneous Worship) – Jonathan David Helser
https://www.youtube.com/
    watch?v=e4ZH11FkkbY&ab_channel=JoshLehman

I Can Hear Your Voice by Michael W Smith
    (Short Version - 3 Minutes)
https://www.youtube.com/watch?v=OwNNfJ-vbnM

I Can Hear Your Voice by Michael W Smith
   (Long Version - 1 Hour)
https://www.youtube.com/watch?v=GrswTKxz8xs

I Can Hear Your Voice by Michael W Smith (Instrumental)
https://www.youtube.com/watch?v=9JFf4sF0cVM

Come Again by Elevation Worship & Maverick City
https://www.youtube.com/watch?v=ZtavurQh8_U

CHAPTER 2 – BEFORE YOUR CREATION

Nothing Else – Rick Pino (feat. Abbie Gamboa) (Live)
https://www.youtube.com/
   watch?v=if0gY1UNKNo&ab_channel=RickPino

Abba (Spontaneous Worship) – Jonathan David Helser
https://www.youtube.com/
   watch?v=e4ZH11FkkbY&ab_channel=JoshLehman

To You (feat. Chandler Moore & Maryanne J. George) | Maverick City Music | TRIBL
https://www.youtube.com/watch?v=dGrXctaw4Bw

Journey – Maryanne J. George (feat. Mitch Wong)
https://www.youtube.com/watch?v=ZexDx5Gprb0&t=3s

CHAPTER 3 – YOU HAVE BEEN CHOSEN

Nothing Else – Rick Pino (feat. Abbie Gamboa) (Live)
https://www.youtube.com/watch?v=if0gY1UNKNo&ab_channel=RickPino

Abba (Spontaneous Worship) – Jonathan David Helser
https://www.youtube.com watch?v=e4ZH11FkkbY&ab_channel=JoshLehman

Mighty Warrior (Weapon of Warfare) – Rick Pino
https://www.youtube.com/watch?v=oP-1BuE5E20

You're an Army – Rick Pino
https://www.google.com/search?q=army+rick+pino

CHAPTER 4 – I AM

Nothing Else – Rick Pino (feat. Abbie Gamboa) (Live)
https://www.youtube.com/watch?v=if0gY1UNKNo&ab_channel=RickPino

Abba (Spontaneous Worship) – Jonathan David Helser
https://www.youtube.com/watch?v=e4ZH11FkkbY&ab_channel=JoshLehman

I Am Your Beloved – Jonathan David Helser & Melissa Helser (Official Lyrics) https://www.youtube.com/watch?v=1cSqRkpeQyM&ab_channel=BethelMusic

Who I Am in Christ, Positive Affirmations – I Am Loved by Stephanie McKenna
https://www.youtube.com/watch?v=KC0BALk9Lzc&t=141s

Who You Say I Am – Hillsong Worship
https://www.youtube.com/watch?v=1Kw6uqtGFfo

You Say – Lauren Daigle (Official Music Video)
https://www.youtube.com/watch?v=sIaT8Jl2zpI

CHAPTER 5 – LIVING FROM THE THRONE ROOM

Nothing Else – Rick Pino (feat. Abbie Gamboa) (Live)
https://www.youtube.com/watch?v=if0gY1UNKNo&ab_channel=RickPino

Abba (Spontaneous Worship) – Jonathan David Helser
https://www.youtube.com/watch?v=e4ZH11FkkbY&ab_channel=JoshLehman

Your (Glory & Priase) – Live Elevation Worship 2017
https://www.youtube.com/watch?v=5aF7nc3-I-U&ab_channel=ElevationWorship

Throne Room Song – Charity Gayle (feat. Ryan Kennedy) (Live)

https://www.youtube.com/watch?v=Xn5n3JKP3sM

I Speak Jesus – Charity Gayle
https://www.youtube.com/watch?v=BRoFayyESfc

Hydrated Soaking Music – Steve Swanson
https://www.youtube.com/watch?v=VAA_HJANPSs

CHAPTER 6 – STRONGHOLDS

Nothing Else – Rick Pino (feat. Abbie Gamboa) (Live)
https://www.youtube.com/watch?v=if0gY1UNKNo&ab_channel=RickPino

Abba (Spontaneous Worship) – Jonathan David Helser
https://www.youtube.com/watch?v=e4ZH11FkkbY&ab_channel=JoshLehman

The Altar Sessions (Live Volume 1 – Full Album) – Rick Pino
https://www.youtube.com/watch?v=FRMOr9uk1Fw&ab_channel=RickPino

You Restore Everything (Live) – Rick Pino
https://www.youtube.com/watch?v=CYxxaUWuEXw

I Speak Jesus – Charity Gayle (feat. Steven Musso)
https://www.youtube.com/watch?v=PcmqSfr1ENY&ab_channel=CharityGayle

He Knows My Name – Francesca Battistelli
(Official Music Video)
https://www.youtube.com/watch?v=jYpBgJHmGmw&ab_channel=FrancescaBattistelli

I Can't Get Away & Downpour – Melissa Helser (feat. Naomi Raine) Live
https://www.youtube.com/watch?v=l2g9iy9th10&ab_channel=BethelMusic

Sound Mind & Turning on the Lights – Melissa Helser
https://www.youtube.com/watch?v=Q4KPRE0vOFo&ab_channel=BethelMusic

CHAPTER 7 – A CHOICE TO HEAL

Nothing Else – Rick Pino (feat. Abbie Gamboa) (Live)
https://www.youtube.com/watch?v=if0gY1UNKNo&ab_channel=RickPino

Abba (Spontaneous Worship) – Jonathan David Helser
https://www.youtube.com/watch?v=e4ZH11FkkbY&ab_channel=JoshLehman

The Altar Sessions (Live Volume 1 – Full Album) – Rick Pino
https://www.youtube.com/watch?v=FRMOr9uk1Fw&ab_channel=RickPino

Learning To Be Loved By You – Melissa Helser
https://www.youtube.com/watch?v=KG7mljj-DsE&ab_channel=CagelessBirds

I Am You Beloved & Running Home – Jonathan David Helser & Melissa Helser (Live)
https://www.youtube.com/watch?v=BaBsx3COdQM&ab_channel=BethelMusic

New Wine – Maverick City Music (Feat. Montel Moore & DOE)
https://www.youtube.com/watch?v=kWOQbxOkKXo&ab_channel=TRIBL

When I Lock Eyes With You – Maverick City and Upperroom
https://www.youtube.com/watch?v=5xvCY0_vaDA&ab_channel=UPPERROOM

The One you Love – Maverick City and Kirk Franklin (feat. Brandon Lake, Dante Bowe & Chandler Moore)
https://www.youtube.com/watch?v=sOM28EW1VRk&ab_channel=TRIBL

Echo In Jesus Name – Charity Gayle (Live)
https://www.youtube.com/watch?v=B33nt6eDBWM

CHAPTER 8 – THROUGH DYING TO SELF

Nothing Else – Rick Pino (feat. Abbie Gamboa) (Live)
https://www.youtube.com/watch?v=if0gY1UNKNo&ab_channel=RickPino

Abba (Spontaneous Worship) – Jonathan David Helser
https://www.youtube.com/watch?v=e4ZH11FkkbY&ab_channel=JoshLehman

Yeshua (Jesus Image) – Michael Koulianos
https://www.youtube.com/watch?v=ivUb1K0B0zE&ab_channel=JesusImage

We Fall Down – Jenn Johnson
https://www.youtube.com/watch?v=Z0fegyKP0b8

I Surrender – Hillsong (feat. Lauren Daigle)
https://www.youtube.com/watch?v=A4N2ausO6Sw&t=66s

CHAPTER 9 – THROUGH INTIMACY

Nothing Else – Rick Pino (feat. Abbie Gamboa) (Live)
https://www.youtube.com/watch?v=if0gY1UNKNo&ab_channel=RickPino

Abba (Spontaneous Worship) – Jonathan David Helser
https://www.youtube.com/watch?v=e4ZH11FkkbY&ab_channel=JoshLehman

Songs of God's Love (Acoustic) – Saddleback Worship

https://www.youtube.com/watch?v=fIm1HKYSzPM&ab_channel=SaddlebackWorship

Penuel (Face to Face) – Rick Pino (Soaking 1.5 Hours)
https://www.youtube.com/watch?v=vz0ghkVSvg0&ab_channel=%D0%91%D0%B8%D0%B7%D0%BD%D0%B5%D1%81%D0%BD%D0%B0%D1%80%D1%83%D0%BA%D0%B0%D1%85%D0%9E%D1%82%D1%86%D0%B0

Touch of Heaven – David Funk (Worship Night)
https://www.youtube.com/watch?v=_fY3l9AKPa0&ab_channel=BethelMusic

CHAPTER 10 – THROUGH THE FRUIT OF THE SPIRIT

Nothing Else – Rick Pino (feat. Abbie Gamboa) (Live)
https://www.youtube.com/watch?v=if0gY1UNKNo&ab_channel=RickPino

Abba (Spontaneous Worship) – Jonathan David Helser
https://www.youtube.com/watch?v=e4ZH11FkkbY&ab_channel=JoshLehman

Refiner – Maverick City Music (feat. Chandler Moore & Steffany Gretzinger)
https://www.youtube.com/watch?v=UGFCbmvk0vo&ab_channel=TRIBL

New Wine – Maverick City Music (Feat. Montel Moore & DOE)
https://www.youtube.com/watch?v=kWOQbxOkKXo&ab_channel=TRIBL

CHAPTER 11 – PREPARING FOR BIRTH

Nothing Else – Rick Pino (feat. Abbie Gamboa) (Live)
https://www.youtube.com/watch?v=if0gY1UNKNo&ab_channel=RickPino

Abba (Spontaneous Worship) – Jonathan David Helser
https://www.youtube.com/watch?v=e4ZH11FkkbY&ab_channel=JoshLehman

The Altar Sessions (Live Volume 1 – Full Album) – Rick Pino
https://www.youtube.com/watch?v=FRMOr9uk1Fw&ab_channel=RickPino

You Restore Everything (Live) – Rick Pino
https://www.youtube.com/watch?v=CYxxaUWuEXw

Learning To Be Loved By You – Melissa Helser
https://www.youtube.com/watch?v=KG7mljj-DsE&ab_channel=CagelessBirds

I Am You Beloved & Running Home – Jonathan David Helser & Melissa Helser (Live)
https://www.youtube.com/watch?v=BaBsx3COdQM&ab_channel=BethelMusic

New Wine – Maverick City Music (Feat.
   Montel Moore & DOE)
https://www.youtube.com/
   watch?v=kWOQbxOkKXo&ab_channel=TRIBL

I Speak Jesus – Charity Gayle (feat. Steven Musso)
https://www.youtube.com/
   watch?v=PcmqSfr1ENY&ab_channel=CharityGayle

When I Lock Eyes With You – Maverick
   City and Upperroom
https://www.youtube.com/
   watch?v=5xvCY0_vaDA&ab_channel=UPPERROOM

He Knows My Name – Francesca Battistelli
   (Official Music Video)
https://www.youtube.com/watch?v=jYpBgJHmGmw&ab_
   channel=FrancescaBattistelli

CHAPTER 12 – IT'S TIME

Nothing Else – Rick Pino (feat. Abbie Gamboa) (Live)
https://www.youtube.com/watch?v=if0gY1UNKNo&ab_
   channel=RickPino

Abba (Spontaneous Worship) – Jonathan David Helser
https://www.youtube.com/watch?v=e4ZH11FkkbY&ab_
   channel=JoshLehman

Earth to God – John Rich

https://www.youtube.com/watch?v=fvMQ_xStg9M&ab_channel=johnrich

Rattle – Elevation Worship (Official Lyric Video)
https://www.youtube.com/watch?v=xrAdbH28gIg&ab_channel=ElevationWorship

Graves Into Gardens – Elevation Worship (feat. Brandon Lake) (Live)
https://www.youtube.com/watch?v=kTvv-9zosPs&ab_channel=musicmeetsheaven

CHAPTER 13 – BUILDING LEGACY

Nothing Else – Rick Pino (feat. Abbie Gamboa) (Live)
https://www.youtube.com/watch?v=if0gY1UNKNo&ab_channel=RickPino

Abba (Spontaneous Worship) – Jonathan David Helser
https://www.youtube.com/watch?v=e4ZH11FkkbY&ab_channel=JoshLehman

Arise (Spontaneous) – Alberto & Kimberly Rivera
https://www.youtube.com/watch?v=XI3WoxPPH9c&ab_channel=KimberlyandAlbertoRivera

Caught Up & His Holy Name (Spontaneous) – Soaking Tunes with Alberto
https://www.youtube.com/watch?v=rwbqS20FTEw&ab_channel=KimberlyandAlbertoRivera

Worthy Of It All – (feat. Anne Dow, Eric Gilmour, Burning Ones, and Raw Encounters)
https://www.youtube.com/watch?v=3BuE85XbSHM&ab_channel=BurningOnes

Famous For (I Believe) & Do It Again (Live) – Tauren Wells (feat. Jenn Johnson & Christine D'Clario)
https://www.youtube.com/watch?v=hLCYTUaoqDM&ab_channel=taurenwellsVEVO

CHAPTER 14 – PASSING THROUGH GENERATIONS

Nothing Else – Rick Pino (feat. Abbie Gamboa) (Live)
https://www.youtube.com/watch?v=if0gY1UNKNo&ab_channel=RickPino

Abba (Spontaneous Worship) – Jonathan David Helser
https://www.youtube.com/watch?v=e4ZH11FkkbY&ab_channel=JoshLehman

Talking to Jesus – Elevation Worship & Maverick City
https://www.youtube.com/watch?v=OXsxw1fRHMA&ab_channel=ElevationWorship

Getting Ready – Maverick City and Upperroom
https://www.youtube.com/watch?v=rcqLmE1vguY&ab_channel=UPPERROOM

We Want More – (feat. John Wilds, Daniel Kolenda,
    Burning Ones, and Raw Encounter)
https://www.youtube.com/
    watch?v=9cyN_FrkkTY&ab_channel=BurningOnes

While listening to God's ordained minstrels is truly a blessing, I encourage you to keep your heart open to hear from Heaven. Papa God desires to place heavenly songs and lyrics in your heart. Special songs and lyrics just for you, to encourage you throughout your day. Spending time in His presence creates an atmosphere for Heavenly Encounter.

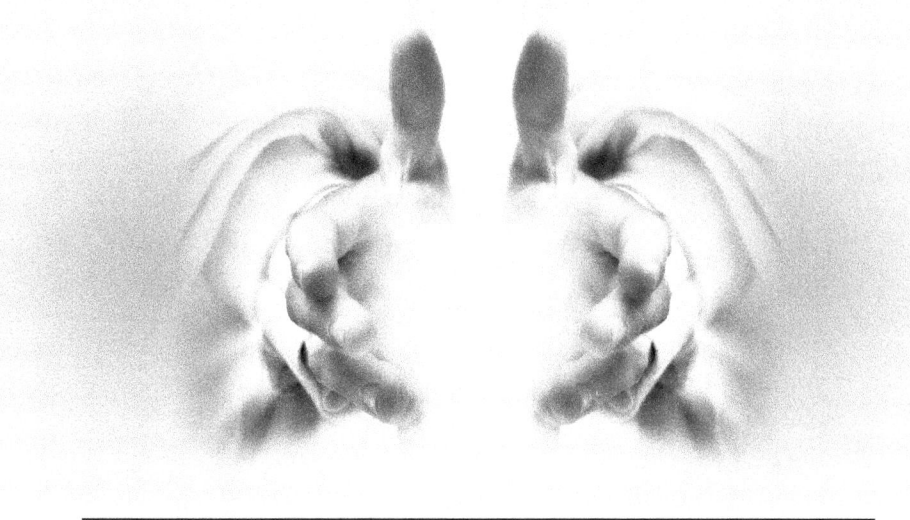

Conclusion

"My Beloved, Before Time…

I Spoke to You…

And You Aligned in Agreement…

Then I placed you in your Mother's womb and sent you to Earth…

For MY Purpose and Glory…

For Such a Time as Now…

My Beloved, 'I SPOKE TO YOU' is a part of our beautiful LOVE Story. As you have read MY Words throughout 'I SPOKE TO YOU,' I have watched you supernaturally and spiritually come alive. Your spirit, soul, and natural man have intertwined and become one IN ME and WITH ME. And I have stirred and ignited the fire within you so that I may use you as a vessel of light for MY GLORY. My Beloved, as our LOVE Story continues to unfold, I know our times of intimacy will only continue to intensify. May MY HEART BEAT for you, My Beloved, and be etched in your heart forever...

I love you, Papa God."

www.ingramcontent.com/pod-product-compliance
Lightning Source LLC
Chambersburg PA
CBHW062055080426
42734CB00012B/2663